RI
TO
GREATER
HEIGHTS

My friend,

You are destined for greatness! Inside of you, God has put seeds of excellence. Those seeds are supposed to grow and flourish. It is so significant to have a positive mindset, especially under these circumstances. So, this book has the potential to completely revolutionize every aspect of your life and career. The sky is no longer the limit but our point of view, so let's all RISE TO GREATER HEIGHTS!

~ DR. NOMPUMELELO REAL KUNENE

Copyright © 2020 Nompumelelo R. Kunene.

All rights reserved. No part of this publication may be reproduced, distributed, or transmitted in any form or by any means, including photocopying, recording, or other electronic or mechanical methods, without the prior written permission of the publisher, except in the case of brief quotations embodied in critical reviews and certain other non-commercial uses permitted by Canadian copyright law. For permission requests, write to the publisher, addressed "Attention: Permissions Coordinator," at the website below.

Published in Seattle, Washington State.

ISBN: 9798637124824

Library of Congress Control Number: 2020907587

This publication is intended to provide accurate and authoritative information regarding the subject matter covered.

First printing edition 2020.

www.risetogreaterheights.com

ORDER YOUR COPY NOW
RISE TO GREATER HEIGHTS
Hardcopy and eBook Widely Available
Click below so you can have immediate access anywhere in the world
Leadership-Empowerment-Purpose Driven-Mentorship
Mental Health-Mindset-Emotional Intelligence
BUSINESS-SCHOOL-COMMUNITY-CHURCH
Order
TODAY
RISE
TO
GREATER
HEIGHTS
For more information:
E-mail: ceo@swaticanadianinternational.ca
Tel: +1(780) 803-5891
Available:
www.swaticanadianinternational.ca
Available on
amazonkindle

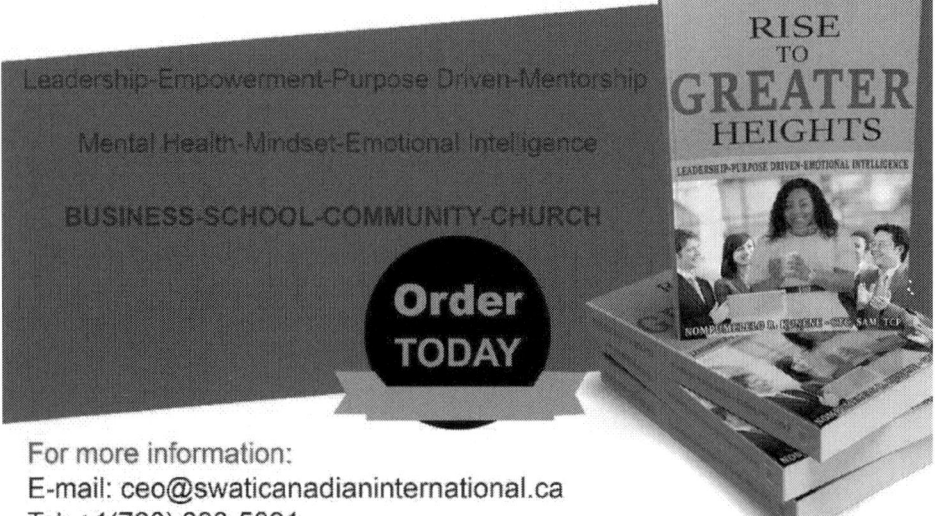

RISE TO GREATER HEIGHTS

Leadership-Empowerment-Purpose Driven Mentorship
Mental Health-Mindset-Emotional Intelligence
Business-School-Community-Church

Nompumelelo Real Kunene, PhD

Table of Contents

FOREWORD by LES BROWN 8
PREFACE 10
ACKNOWLEDGMENTS 13
INTRODUCTION 15
WHAT'S HOLDING YOU BACK? 20
CHASE AFTER SUCCESS 28
GROW YOUR BUSINESS 40
OVERCOME BUSINESS OBSTACLES 51
WORK-LIFE BALANCE 64
CULTIVATE YOUR MINDSET 73
FOR SUCCESS 73
SOLID MENTAL HEALTH 81
EMOTIONAL INTELLIGENCE 91
EFFECTIVE LEADERSHIP 101
EMPOWERMENT 113
MENTORSHIP AND COACHING 133
STRATEGIES FOR GROWING YOUR CHURCH 145
WAYS TO TRUST GOD WITH YOUR TROUBLES 153
CAN SINGLE PARENTS BE SUCCESSFUL? 161
MAKE A DIFFERENCE TO THE VULNERABLE 173
RESILIENCE TO GREATNESS 185
REFERENCES 190
ABOUT THE AUTHOR 193
RESOURCES 200

FOREWORD by LES BROWN

If you are stuck in a dead-end job or your first time attempting to start your own business, perhaps you were laid off and are not sure of what to do next? Rise to Greater Heights by Nompumelelo Kunene is the book for you. Hi, my name is Les Brown international motivational speaker and trainer. I highly recommend Rise to Greater Heights for entrepreneurs, executives, and professionals. Ms. Kunene is a powerhouse of a young lady. I really respect her tenacity and determination in taking charge of her destiny. It has been said that success leaves clues. Nompumelelo has shared the many lessons she has learned along her road to success as an entrepreneur.

She has a very witty and straightforward approach on how to tap into your human potential. She helps you to identify the things that hold you back from taking a chance on your own talents and abilities. I have a saying, "you don't have to be great to get started but you have to get started to be great." Nompumelelo gives you tips on how to get beyond procrastination and fear of success. How to overcome mental blocks such as analysis paralysis. That is when you over analyze your work and never get started on building your business. She shares how important it is to hold yourself to a higher standard because your team will mirror your efforts.

Ms. Kunene shares so many gems for personal and professional success. The importance of realizing you fail your way to success. Failure is a tool for learning. Way too often people quit on themselves not realizing that anything worth achieving will take time and a relentless effort. Oftentimes, people will criticize and ridicule that which they are afraid of attempting so it's important to block out external and internal critics. Ms. Kunene offers some techniques to help block out the naysayers and self doubt. Nompumelelo has written a blueprint for achieving success. If you are looking to take your business to the next level, Rise to Greater Heights is a must read! You have greatness within you, that is my story and I am sticking to it.

LES BROWN
World's Leading Motivational Speaker
"IT'S POSSIBLE"

PREFACE

The coronavirus plague is not just a pandemic, it's also a global epidemic that has compelled countries to lockdown (including Canada), shut schools and public places and put our life on hold. Coronavirus disease (COVID-19) is a contagious disease which is the severe critical respiratory disorder that can proliferate from person to person. Nobody predicted that it would kill so many people, quarantine and self-isolation at the personal level was then established to prevent spreading illness. Over the month of March, the coronavirus hit us by blow and has significantly worsened, life has radically changed around the world.

Life is undoubtedly full of surprises; my heart goes to people who live in a noxious situation at home and to all those with recession and other concerns that is making social distancing difficult. As regular practices change and the world adapts to a new normal, please be strong, and let us brave through this together. While quarantined starting March 16, 2020, I started journaling this book "Rise to Greater Heights" and remained confident in the direction of my dreams. During this chaos, I appreciated the importance of humankind, then chose to concentrate on the positive so that I have the strength and rally further with purpose and hope.

The COVID-19 pandemic brought travel to a standstill, depriving my company hundreds of dollars in lost revenue. As a corporate travel consultant, I work with thousands of hotel, restaurant and tourism operators across the country who are now distressed by the pandemic and unexpectedly forced to close unless if hotels are providing rooms for humanitarian purposes such as accommodation for health-care workers. Taking a snapshot of clients, I've lost is difficult, and the federal wage subsidy program provides some relief for the tourism industry that only expires in three months. The cancellation of business conferences and conventions across the country has walloped my company because we are tourism-dependent agency. Certain measures are not helping, but to issue vouchers for future travel instead of a refund for our clients.

In the case of COVID-19, we've been asked to stay home, stay away from others and practice hand hygiene in order to lessen the probability of infection, flatten the curve and reduce social disruption among Canadians. Corona has brought with it a surge of depressing outcomes, some might even feel that it's a violation of their individual right, being made to stay home. However, when it comes to the greater good, the curse of this coronavirus has become a blessing for me, and I have used this opportunity to be courageous in writing this book. In the wake of the pandemic corona virus (COVID-19), when the world stop moving, and stuck with my two beautiful munchkins at home, "Rise to Greater Heights" book was born. Rise to Greater Heights was born from my experience of wearing different hats in life. I have had the chance to lead, be led by, or watch others leadership from afar.

ACKNOWLEDGMENTS

First and foremost, all the praises belong to God almighty, for breathing words of wisdom into my ears and his showers of blessings throughout my journaling to complete this book successfully. Writing a book is indeed a process and more satisfying than I could have ever imagined.

I am astounded in all humility and gratitude to acknowledge my strength to all leaders who had faith in me and allowed me to empower their team with a fresh perspective inspiration they require to pursue success. To all the folks I have had the chance to lead, be led by, or watch their leadership from afar, I want to say thank you for being the inspiration and foundation for my book. I am grateful to all of those with whom I have had the pleasure to share my life with, they kept me going on and this book would not have been feasible without their input in my life. I am thankful that the Lord placed you in my life to have helped me to put these ideas, well above the level of simplicity and into something tangible, each of you have provided me broad personal and professional support.

Writing a book is harder than I thought, having a thought and transforming it into a book is as hard as it sounds. I would like to convey my deep and heartfelt gratefulness to my pastors, church family (both in Canada and Eswatini) for their love, prayers, sacrifices and continuing support. Nobody has been more valuable to me in the pursuit of this book than the members of my family who provide unending inspiration. Any attempt at any level can't be satisfactorily completed without the support and guidance of you my loving family.

Without the experiences and support from my friends and network, this book would not exist. You never got tired of me bothering you to proofread my chapters, thank you! I'm forever indebted to my editors for their journalistic help, eager understanding, and ongoing support in bringing my stories to life. It is because of their hard work and reassurance that I have a legacy to pass on to my loved ones where one didn't exist before. Finally, I am also thankful that you managed to get yourself a copy of "Rise to Greater Heights" today, trust me you won't be disappointed.

INTRODUCTION

This book is a comprehensive guide to turn your fears into greater success while seizing new opportunities. Setting your mindset for success is significant, thus, this book has the potential to completely revolutionize every aspect of your life and career. You can also buy this book for a family member or a relative who needs that inspiration to face the world with a positive mindset.

The fear of rising above mediocrity is often something that develops without our conscious awareness. Still, we can identify why our fear is formed in the first place and work to bring about change intentionally. Being here shows you are not willing to settle for a mediocre life, so don't let others stand in the way of your dreams. Starting your own business can be a scary thing, though it also opens a world of almost infinite opportunities each day. What you can do to get your venture beyond the clear sustenance point is not concentrating on the short-term result of your work. The success of your small business depends on your hard work to expand revenues using several approaches.

While many of us acknowledge the damage that comes from crippling fears, it's only human to wonder whether you'll be up to the challenge. We know that fear can also influence us to take precautionary measures and prevent us from difficult things. A small, fearful part of us would prefer not to take the risk. Our longing to succeed competently can push us to set apart our well-being and discovering the right stability can feel irresistible. Therefore, establishing balanced work-life assimilation is crucial, though, more and more people are finding it hard to effectively accomplish their responsibilities both at home and in the workplace.

Fear of rising against all the odds is easy to miss. Sometimes you can find yourself on the edge of significant achievement. Still, you noticed things starting to go wrong because this looks a lot like garden-variety delay and anxiety. Setting your mindset for success is significant. I think that our opinions have an amazing influence on our daily lives because we all want a successful, happy life. Good mental health is not merely the lack of psychological wellbeing problems, and it's a generally recognized fact that adults spend most of their lives at work. Powers associated with emotional intelligence play a large part in the success of managers, as well as having practical situational knowledge can be a potent tool for leading a team.

Some people become overpowered by fear and want to stay away from circumstances that might make them worried. Being clear-eyed about our efforts is the first step to working through them. It can be challenging to break this cycle but, you are about to uncover and build new aspects of your personality. A great leader is always capable of leading a team to higher achievement. Managers who show excellent leadership traits can encourage their teams to achieve incredible things, irrespective of the situation that they are facing. If you manage other people, the first thing you need to know is that your accomplishment depends on their success. High-scoring managers inspire their teams by communicating information, asking for their feedback, and prevent micromanaging.

Cultivating your team's progress is a characteristic of great leadership that pays instant and long-term surpluses. When handled in an effective and productive approach, new heights of efficiency and success can be reached. Development requires all hands-on-deck, so creating a strategic plan to map out the steps to get there is how a concept is attained. The people in your team must also be prepared to acknowledge changes. Lastly, be responsible for your actions and responsibilities to succeed.

NOTES

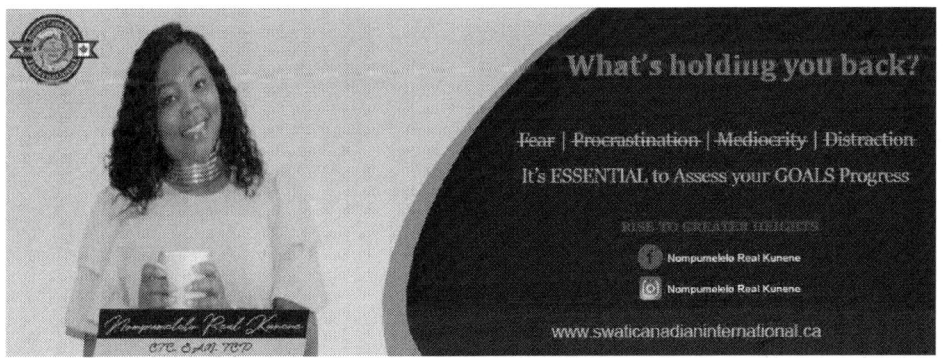

Chapter 1

WHAT'S HOLDING YOU BACK?

There are many reasons why people don't reach their dreams. You must understand the issues that keep you away from achieving your potential success. It's good to know what is keeping you away from your dreams, as you can try to change the way that you approach them! Once you identify the reasons why you are being held back from reaching your goals, you can then try and work on it and improve. People do not devote to their visions and delay the fulfilment of their ideas, which could probably be keeping them back from achieving their dreams. The good thing is that you can conquer the motives if you recognize them, so, keep reading to find out the top things that may be holding you back, instead of rejecting the truth.

There is an added level to the anxiety of success, and many of us are accustomed to think that the road to achievement entails risks. I do not doubt that you have tried to pursue your ambitions. Establishing and attaining big goals can be challenging. We all have dreams that we are so eager to accomplish in our careers but feel like something is standing in the way, which threatens to lead to disappointment. We have suppressed that reaction and believe that we don't deserve success. Still, you need to battle for greater efficiency and make the most of your objectives, which requires you to concentrate on the end outcome.

Fight for better achievements. Many people leave their goals halfway just because they can't keep up the drive, so you must understand that the people who care don't matter and that this is your own life! Don't associate accomplishment with awkward things such as a race with others but enjoy without bothering yourself about what others might think of you. Go for your goals and be successful, by breaking down your big ambition into smaller, more feasible tasks. Be characterized by your robust determination, and to do that, you must be confident about the measures you are taking. Therefore, fight for your visions by doing the things you enjoy so that you can become a precise model of unbelievable success.

Fear
All those accrued worries can undoubtedly convert into fears, but this is something that you are personally allowing it to happen to prevent you from accomplishing your desires. It's easy to be afraid of being judged and being concerned about what others think; it stops you from acting and making you scared of taking the critical action. The age-old adversary, fear is one of the motives behind why we don't go for what we need in life. Almost undoubtedly, fear is a significant element in stopping many of you from chasing after your dreams. Being worried about everything is what paralyzes you, because you may be concerned about going for something. Then you fear people judging you for it, which prevents you from acting. As a result, fear is what holds you back. It is the feeling of ambiguity that makes you scared of taking the initial step to success.

> "Whenever I am afraid, I will trust in You" (Psalms 56:3 NKJV HolyBible, 2020).

You might have to ask yourself if: fear, ridicule, pain, rejection, disappointment, or mediocrity is what is holding you from going confident in the direction of your dreams. Stop allowing your fears to keep you back. The only solution that cures your worries is action, so go for your goals and succeed! You should know that you are an overcomer who've been called for greatness, so rise to greater heights because you are the chosen one. You must understand that the opinions of people who care do not matter. Every time you delay meeting your fears, you automatically postpone the recognition of achieving your goals. For this reason, you should be doing the things you love, and only through decisive action can you enter your zone of discomfort and develop your comfort area.

This is your own life, so live without fretting about what others might think of you. Don't let others stand in the direction of your desires. Having made the initial move during the vanishment of your fears will make you achieve your potential goals if you don't quit. You are almost halfway in the direction of your dreams. You'll undoubtedly be amazed to see that most people are only concerned about themselves and are not criticizing you at all.

Procrastination
From the very get-go when you get hold of your idea, setting things off till forever shows that you are indeed keeping yourself away from your goals. You're not pretty sure of what you're waiting for, and it seems like you are anticipating for some miracle. Unfortunately, there is no right time, as much as you might try and wait for one. If you discover that you procrastinate a lot when it comes to taking the measures to accomplish your goals, your ambition stays as nothing more than a dream. Putting ideas off can only hold you back from your vision, so get started right away because there won't be an excellent time to achieve your concept than now.

Don't delay and kick yourself later. You are one step nearer to reaching your goals. Every single minute is a chance. You can't postpone the starting time to achieve a goal that you waited for because that day will never come. Avoid allowing your procrastination to keep you away from achieving your goals. Spend some time to do a little research on how to overcome delays. Once you have done this, you should find yourself procrastinating a lot less.

Lack of vision and full of doubts
If you do not have a clear idea of what ambitions you want to reach about, you generally end up with a massive mixture of worries. Stop doubting yourself. You are smarter than you imagine; therefore, start taking the steps you need to do to attain your end goal. A vision gives you the plan you need in the direction of your goals. Still, if you stick to what you believe is appropriate and are not open to any various concepts, you may become disappointed when you don't progress. Aim not to remain in the same form of attitude. This is the portion where you put in the work to lay a strategy on paper with the actions you need to take and considering what do you need to do to reach your goals. It's always good to know what it is that you want, and having an open mind, will allow you to become closer to accomplishing your dreams by learning more from others.

Giving up to soon
There are certain things in life where it seems like going on is next to impossible, and too many people set a big goal but feel disheartened when this goal is not met straight away. When you give up on your ambitions straight away because they are taking too much time, it can cause you to miss out on achieving the impossible. If you are impatient and anticipate outcomes right away, you are not going to accomplish many of your goals. When you're already swamped, you must keep in mind that achieving your goals is a big success. We all hit moments when it's easy to tell yourself to give up, but you never know how soon you will begin to see improvement if you hang in there. Be easygoing and look forward to achieving your result. If you conquer these things, you give yourself the best opportunity of chasing your goals successfully. This is about becoming more in

harmony with your deeper self because you cannot produce if you are not true to yourself.

"The future rewards those who press on. I don't have time to feel sorry for myself. I don't have time to complain. I'm going to press on" (Barack Obama, 2011).

Distraction

There's a way you'll need to take before you can accomplish your goals. Still, every time you lose motivation, it kills your probability of success. Every single achievement is about attention, but when we spread our concentration too much, we diffuse our dedication. Remaining committed is essential while working on your vision. Still, distraction is undoubtedly one of the worst enemies of young entrepreneurs of diverse spheres. When you are dragged in different ways, your focus disappears, and you can simply find yourself lacking motivation. Deciding to act following your goals is the only way to remain positive and continually produce the results of high excellence. Instead of indulging in events that only bring momentary pleasure, stay dedicated to all the awareness focused on the current workflow.

Lack of Belief

The absence of having faith in the opportunities of pursuing your ambitions will undoubtedly hold you back, and you are more likely to be subjected to a lack of confidence, which will lead you to stop trying. Doubting yourself can hold you back from living a beautiful life, and what goes on in our subconscious mind has an impact on our actions. Setting apart your restricting attitudes into touch will go a long path to pursuing your goals. You will find yourself moving closer to your desires without anything stopping you. To help you in your purpose of pursuing your ambitions, you need to ask yourself questions that are going to help and inspire you even more to achieve your goals.

Assess Mistakes and Review Progress

Goals, by their very nature, take a while to accomplish. It's common knowledge that envisioning your potential can be valuable in terms of making your aspirations and desires come alive. But if we don't evaluate our missteps, we won't know why we are not accomplishing what we want to succeed. When we go back and look at our journey, we will be able to see what we have done amiss. However, if you don't have timely and actionable criticism, then you won't know what's working and what's worth it. Therefore, it's essential to reassess your goal progress. After all, you don't know what you're fighting for until you really think about it.

Any person who is competent in consistently attaining their goals is also regularly evaluating their purposes, but if you devote too much time fantasizing, your brain sees the big endgame without seeing the difficulties. When you can reflect on what is going amiss, and you can try again to find a way out of the dilemma instead of repeating the same errors. Avoid allowing your not evaluating your growth hold you back. After all, it's easier to reach your purpose if you have a road map to measure your faults. It's essential to have goals and to make changes early, so you stay on track. Overall, yes, evaluating your purposes regularly allows you to know the direction that you want to go.

NOTES

Chapter 2

CHASE AFTER SUCCESS

The way to your success isn't always easy to discover, but you can do a lot more than you think, and none of this means that the search isn't valuable. Moving towards your visions isn't always all it's thought up to be. Even with trials in the way, you can tell that you'll get there in the end. You're vigorously stepping in the direction of reaching your dreams, and it can be tough. There may be instants of hesitation but never give up. Instead, learn how to have confidence in your thoughts and make them come true today. Don't give up on your desires; just recall this in case you don't find your way: you can have the drive within you to get what you want. This universe functions rather inversely, and everything that you need doesn't come easy, so please don't pay attention to the worrywarts.

Dreams are the desires of our intuitive. Visualize a universe in which you know what your vision is, and the idea of following your dreams often looks more gratifying. But deep down, it's the confidence within you that will keep you working in the direction of your dreams. You might have received results that say that you didn't make it. Don't be discouraged by the results you received; go confident in the direction of your dreams. Believe in your dreams that one day it will become a reality, and it doesn't matter how long it takes for you to reach your destiny. Never give up in life, never give up in your dream and keep your dream alive.

As you work to accomplish your most determined goals, here are few motives why you've got to have faith in yourself that will ignite the spark which keeps you focused:

Identify Goals
Start by writing your goals down and use every minute of belief to fuel yourself by doing something that makes you feel content and holds your interest. Goals give us a way to measure our development and to act towards your dreams. The most challenging part is recognizing the goals you want to follow because the vision of your life is your utmost strength. The goal is to make incremental changes to your lifestyle, so you may need to discover diverse opportunities to see what sticks and what doesn't. Life should not be dreary; your goals and drives can change and transform over time, so make it a good one and use it prudently!

Be True to Yourself
The reality is, your journey to be a better person starts with you, as you make the change from being an idle bum to someone who acts. Knowing who you are at your core will make you understand that you are the only one who can accomplish your dreams, so be in full control of your life. If you have a dream, conduct yourself like you have faith in your powerful voice, and it will echo throughout the universe. If there's anything humankind has learned about behaviors is that, who you are and will become is 100% down to you, so don't turn back around and never give up. Treat every phase towards your visions as an achievement.

Embrace Transformation
Curveballs will continually be coming in your direction. Still, you will see tests as opportunities to learn, as you pursue your dream. You need to disregard all negative attitudes to overcome nervousness and wrath that create struggles within your relationships. Letting go of unpopular opinions allows you to turn out to be the best version of yourself, which will help you to heal emotionally and gives you peace. Fake it until you make it as you attract different conducts of

moving towards your dream and push yourself to keep moving forward.

Positive Thinking
It's all about your mindset. Once you have your mind set on success, it will vigorously be focused on discovering opportunities. You might have moments when you want to throw in the towel. Still, I urge you to overcome your doubts by analyzing all possible consequences and notice more possibilities on what you can do to move forward. So, if you exercise constructive thinking and fake your confidence in yourself long enough, you can be able to contest all the challenges and delays you come across.

Spark Your Imagination and Motivation
You need to believe in yourself to get going and keep your dreams top of mind as you reach each momentous to inspire you to push forward. To keep the momentum, you need to work your style and be conscious that you are in your way. Following your dreams will give you purpose to see your goals through and understand that you do have everything you need to reach your full potential.

Develop A Routine
We all have days when we wake up just not feeling it but surprise yourself by pushing yourself outside of your comfort zone. Life is filled with unpredicted twists, and from time to time, the right path isn't always clear. Goals encourage us to stay on track. You might have discovered something new about yourself, therefore, letting yourself to produce over time is an essential part of life. It's significant to understand that disappointments are a natural part of life and fear of achieving hides in our intuitive.

Good Habits

You might have instants when you no longer have faith in your dreams, but a key component in rising as an individual is learning to accept personal accountability. Developing a practice takes time and replication. We can't help being frightened of change because the unknown is always a little terrifying but remember that even small habits can have increasing consequences. You should always take new habits and activities slow, which will keep you taking baby steps on the right track. Building robust and consistent practices will withstand you through lacklustre eras to shake things up in your life.

Community

The community has been recognized to be one of the most influential assets for generating transformation. It provides us with support and connection to other like-minded people. You don't have to go on this ride alone. You must find ways to be part of a community where people connect through shared ideas, ethics, views, and serving to improve the lives of those around you.

Listen

Being an active listener can transform your life for the better and paying attention to podcasts has a similar outcome on your brain as reading books. Listening allows you to grow closer influences on others by developing more exceptional relationships and worldviews outside our own experiences.

Live with Integrity

Individual integrity is a foundation of who we are and what we stand for. No matter how discouraged you might get at times, make sure you take the time to comprehend what honesty means to you. Living with integrity means being factual to your standards and always have everything in you to make it come to pass.

Recognize the Journey

The path to success is an ongoing journey, so don't turn away from new opportunities or avoid your errands. Know that not everything in life is not straight and quickly done, be eager to take a chance and push yourself outside of your comfort zone. It's time to stretch yourself, strive to keep learning new things to develop, and become an experienced person.

Stay Motivated

The only rule you should be mindful of is that you oversee your life when you admit that you alone are in control of your actions, and your dreams must come from within yourself. To take this a step further, keep your drive burning by taking time every day to reignite that core flame for becoming the person you want to be.

Purpose has much more optimistic implications than luck, and this means that achieving accomplishment in any field of endeavour is foreseeable, so what we think, we become. You might have a receive negative results about what you're dreaming of becoming. You might have failed an examination required for your designation, but never be discouraged about what the lessons you learned from that failure. The results that you got does not determine your destiny. You're called for greatness; you will go confident, trusting your God to lead you in your greatness.

> *"The mind feasts on what it focuses on. What consumes my thinking will be the making or the breaking of my identity"*
> *(Lysa TerKeust, 2016).*

Our destiny is not something we can sit by and let happen to us. Still, the purpose is a series of opportunities that allow us to learn lessons and advance our awareness. Decisions are the hardest thing to make, and your state of mind is the stirring power behind the decisions you make. Nelson Mandela once said, *"May your choices reflect your hopes, not your fears" (Nelson Mandela, 2008)*. We need to act on the opportunities we are offered with fate. Then we will certainly accomplish the achievement we imagined for our lives. I believe we are in full control of our choices, and the thing that fuels destiny-shaping decisions is our state of awareness. Abilities such as courage and endurance can all help to transform your destiny, which means that if you make the right choices and take the right actions, it may open doors for you.

Destiny is commonly regarded as fate, yet it's the top tier in the outstanding structure of opportunities. Our thoughts shape our reality; thus, destiny is our potential waiting to happen. Start today, at this moment, at this hour, to become what do you have dreamt of being several years ago. Continue to be the person that you wanted to be from your childhood; in that career that you have wished to practice. It is high time, and it is a wake-up call that you start working on becoming the person that you've dreamt to be years ago. If you're not doing it, somebody else will do it for themselves. Somebody else will climb up the ladder of success. You know that under the right surroundings, you could go far, *knowing who you are and who you desire to be will remain the keys to your victory*. As you go through life and work toward your dreams, make sure you position yourself on a track to becoming who you want to be.

We're our own worst adversaries when it comes to reaching success. Still, with the right attitude and a little bit of leadership, we will know that we are capable of great things. Success isn't about being hurled into the stratosphere instant. It's an APPROACH you take on to accomplish your goals. Goals give us a path in our lives and living a life that's full of hunger and drive. Some of us are self-destructive without recognizing it, and most people live their lives waiting for something to materialize. They lack the ambition to be a go-getter, and others are aware of the fact but lack the knowledge to advance. The truth is achievement isn't a goal or the end. It's about taking steady action, trying different possibilities, and seeing the outcomes. By now, you should have written a business plan, working on a business idea, could've started networking with prospective clients, but you're failing to manage your time. Sleep is for rich people, and rest cannot make you realize your dreams. Whatever dream you have cannot be a reality if you sleep more than hustle. You should be the one controlling your own time, not the other way around.

TIPS FOR MANAGING YOUR TIME WISELY

Make a "To Do" list to run the day
Part of the key to time management is just staying in charge and be sure to keep track of everything that's taking up your time.

Plan Your Time
Start by making goals and give yourself a manageable range of time how you want to accomplish your goals. Keep a separate list of things you would like to get done and do not start your business day until you get to the business. Now that you know where your time is going look at your week and assign tasks for each day and rank your goals in the order in which you would like to complete them.

Set Specific Goals
Goal setting is crucial to any good time management strategy, and if you don't have clear goals, it can be hard to stay on track. Without goals that you're working toward, you might find yourself overwhelmed and not know where to begin. You'll do your best when

you have clear goals in mind to make sure you're participating in events that boost your business goals.

Realize that your time is valuable and learn to say NO
It's easy in a culture like ours to over-obligate yourself, so don't let your agenda to fill up with things that don't get you closer to your goals. Being too keen to please can be risky, it can take all that time to back out of it, so do not feel guilt-tripped into doing something you don't want to do. You can't instantly say yes to proposals that sound impressive, but if something seems like a waste of your time, don't indulge yourself. Appreciate your boundaries and learn to say no, without feeling uncomfortable.

Track Your Time
Time tracking is a beneficial tool to help you determine just how to prioritize which order to tackle your concerns and begin working on them systematically.

Reward Yourself
Be eager to please yourself if you've achieved some goals or become more dedicated to your responsibilities. You need to be grateful for who you have become and enjoy the fruits of your hard work. Give yourself a small incentive to appreciate what you've achieved.

"I have no regrets" (Justin Trudeau, 2016).
You may be sitting here wondering why you are the only one experiencing struggle when it looks easy for everyone else to achieve what they want. Perhaps you don't need me to tell you that life is intrinsically hard, and the influence of positive thinking is at the base of our existence. It's hard to establish lifelong relationships with others, and many of us have learned to suppress our battles because society tends to focus on visible behavior. Misery is everywhere and

unavoidable, it's hard to find work that gives your life value and that you're good at. We haven't been taught to overlook the certainty that visible behaviors (i.e., criticalness) are indicators of internal battles. Whether you're dealing with economic challenges or work-related matters, struggles have always been linked with being ineffective. Struggles have been looked back in bad remorse. Yet, they are inevitable, but what many tend to disregard is that these problematic encounters are natural parts of our lives. Conquering life's battles is never easy, but these instants help us flourish.

Affliction is also a key theme in the Bible, but when encountered with hardship, thrive to move forward and push towards the next level of progress and revolution. At Times it may even seem unethical, but the bible tells us of many cases where God was also involved in suffering. "who Himself bore our sins in His own body on the tree, that we, having died to sins, might live for righteousness— by whose stripes you were healed" (I Peter 2:24 NKJV HolyBible, 2020).

This reveals that even Jesus himself suffered for our sins. Though this may be true, some struggle more than others, but Jesus endured the most significant prejudice of all when He died for sinners like you and me. So, in instants, when we're hurting for no apparent justification, we should reassure ourselves understanding that any worthwhile achievement is developed through struggle.

Hold your head up high and run unto what the psalmist wrote, "Give thanks to the Lord, for He is good; His love endures forever" (Psalm 107:1 NKJV HolyBible, 2020). We cannot underestimate the value of surrounding ourselves with positive thinkers, because these individuals promoted positive thinking to comprehensiveness by inspiring individuals to concentrate on their strengths. To rise from your struggles, you need a magnet-like charm to bring others into the battle and triumph a united effort. You need people in your life who can change the way you think, and these incredible human beings are going to hold you accountable. You can do better than the existing customs you are living too, so being able to motivate and inspire others is a great strength.

NOTES

GROW
YOUR BUSINESS
Strategic Partnerships
Customer Service & Loyalty
Niche Market | Market Conditions
Social Media | Networking
Growth requires all hands on deck
RISE TO GREATER HEIGHTS
Nompumelelo Real Kunene
RISE TO GREATER HEIGHTS
Nompumelelo Real Kunene
Nompumelelo Real Kunene
www.swaticanadianinternational.ca

Chapter 3

GROW YOUR BUSINESS

Expanding a small business isn't simple. Growing it is often a requirement for your business's existence, and you must invest time if you're looking to gain the benefits. Learning how to develop your business isn't just a worthwhile objective. It is one of the hardest challenges many come across when they are thinking of getting out of the 9 – 5 daily routines. Still, after that, it's merely a matter of acting and laying in the effort to measure. Like anything else in life or business, speedy development doesn't occur overnight, so creating sincere benefit and consider helping your clients should be the foundation. Every facet of your company deserves to be noticed to turn it into the income-generating dynamo you imagined. From employee coaching to marketing, there are numerous successful steps to follow if you wish to see your business expand.

Strategic Partnerships
Once you've made a choice that you want your business to expand, the next step is to find partnerships. Strategic partnerships with the right companies can make a world of change. Collaboration can be as easy as an unofficial deal between businesses in complementary markets to recommend clients for each other. Many potential growth approaches are accessible to you, so look out for companies that are complementary to your own and offer opportunities for working together. If you are a trusted advisor in your field, you can create your distinctive blend of approaches to share your expertise freely to establish different products. What's vital is to test yourself any time you encounter, offering deals disguised as something more valuable. Be mindful in choosing a method that's a perfect fit for your entire

strategic proposal. As mentioned, this simplified development approach of pursuing alliances with other businesses can let you reach a broad range of consumers swiftly.

Understand Customer Service
You can only build products and services that will be a massive hit if you know your customer's needs and create products and services that meet those needs. One avenue to know precisely what your customers need is by customizing your services and encouraging them to give feedback. You can also get an understanding of your clients through research and reviews, which proves you are attentive to the desires of your customers and expectations. You should be continually encouraging them to provide honest reviews. Still, it will be challenging to meet your customer's needs if you don't deliver quality customer service. Reviews are the best way to get inside the mind of your customers; this part of the business is about taking the additional measure to make them feel special.
Let your customers know that they are valued; this makes it easier for you to acquire products and services that are appropriate to the current needs of the market. If your customers have difficulties, make sure you tackle them right away, it helps you identify the areas in which your business needs to enhance. Your clients will not only remember excellent service, but they will also be more prone to refer other people to you. So, take time to respond to their concerns in a good way. Have plans in place to cultivate current customers, because if they find the customer service satisfactory, they might even advise others to also buy from your business. Be sure to go the extra mile when you can. Above all, make sure your customer service is outstanding, and customers should not feel like things are challenging for them if they bring up specific concerns.

Establish Customer Loyalty

It takes time to inspire customers to come and buy what you have to offer. Thus, loyalty options are good ways to boost sales. It costs up to three times more money to obtain new customers than it does to provide something to an active customer. Developing brand recognition in your local neighborhood is a great way to entice new business. It's not enough to just get customers to buy, think about partaking in a community event to boost your business profile. Think About that other competitors could offer customers better service, creating customer loyalty points will help you keep customers. Don't feel satisfied just because you already have a lot of reliable customers. If there's a clear motivation to spend more money with you, it'll pay off in the long run. Develop an appealing loyalty program and let these most loyal customers be the first ones to know. Offer loyalty incentives and make them available to your existing customers and watch sales rise steeply over time. This is because your customers can be easily attracted to other options. Thus, obtaining new customers is pricey; you need to promote loyalty to make sure that your customers know they are valued.

Conquer a Niche Market

Make sure you've clearly outlined your plan's scope, remember the analogy of the big fish in the small pond? The niche market is the pond, so you should observe where your customers are coming from to determine whether your marketing activities are profitable or not. Enhance your method if something is not working, and this can direct you into a shared line of business or a completely different one. Don't allow new developments to cut into your revenue scope. Concentrate your time on the actions that attain the best outcomes, which is how this approach for expanding your business works. Don't be skeptical of research. You can also acquire new products to sell to your existing market or a closely identified group of customers. As mentioned, think of the narrowly defined group as a subgroup of the bigger niche market, and don't be afraid to charge your client for adjustments.

Consider Market Conditions

You should think about market circumstances. For example, if your new market comprises of a younger demographic, acquisition might be the best approach if you choose to grow into a new geographic position where you need connections and local understanding. An acquisition may also be a good plan when you think of expanding your business. Still, your potential company is underestimated; this approach will give you a recognized clientele and venture that you can adapt to add significance. Purchasing an alternative business might be a lucrative approach to boost market share. Still, the first thing that most likely comes to mind is finding new customers. Therefore, it's easier and more cost-effective to get people who are already buying from you to buy more because the customers you already have are your best bet for increasing your sales.

Diversify Your Business Consistently

Look into changing your deals and make sure the information you're providing is consistent across the board. Finding new uses for your services is an excellent tactic to attract existing customers, so pick one or two of these concepts that are appropriate to your business and get busy enhancing your growth strategy. Although you possibly won't encounter expansion right away, you must think about growth. Pinpoint new prospects within your niche, whichever method of growing your business you choose, you will see improvement if you keep at it. To grow, discover the uncomfortable goals and will effectively transform your business into all you want it to be.

Maximize Social Media

Without a doubt, social media is a compelling tool to boost your business to prospective customers. Your business must have something it is enthusiastic about to get significant awareness across social listening. Beyond social listening, you can discover out what consumers are saying about you, and this helps in enhancing the view of your business. Paying close attention to what people say and reading their comments will give you a notion on how to make them feel more content. Then gain an understanding of their actions and developments that appeal to your target market and enhance your customer service. Make sure your business is involved in social media. You must ensure your business exists to connect to the community, not for more than just making money. This helps you stay relevant, so discover keywords social media to improve building your business outline and appeal to new customers.

Franchising

If you have a profitable enterprise, contracting your business can be a successful development approach. While franchise expenses are high and turning to a contract model is complicated, but if you have a successful strategy that can be undoubtedly copied by others. You're certainly considering expanding fast, so look at franchising it. The rumors of entrepreneurs who have turned out to be both well-known due to contracting their small businesses are legendary. Franchising may be the rapid path for growing your business, and it could make all the change if you're genuinely exploring options for quick development. There are numerous avenues of expanding your business by making your product or service accessible to a new group of customers, and the achievement of your business also relies on the value of employees that you hire. On the other hand, in certain conditions, it may be less expensive to grow your current business than to pay a substantial percentage for a costly acquisition. Under this strategy, your company looks to secure a more significant portion of your current market with the products it already has.

Participate in Networking Events

Spend time to develop your networks, trade shows can be an excellent approach to expand, so if granted an opportunity to join these events, take it. Networking allows you to develop contacts with other individuals and trade shows bring people who are already involved in the type of product or service you offer. This is the chance to broaden your networks, but the trick is to pick the trade shows you want to join in wisely. As expressed, networking is a better approach to connect with folks who can impressively enhance your base line and encourage them to refer customers to you through word of mouth.

"Two are better than one, because they have a good reward for their labor" (Ecclesiastes 4:9 NKJV HolyBible, 2020).

Hosting Your Own Event

Hosting your own event or webinar can be a perfect path to get to understand your clients and promote any product or service. Events can also motivate you to *expand any business fast*, so encourage some of your amazing existing customers to come and bring their friends. But one of the best and most efficient ways to develop a business swiftly is to create an email list, as they deliver a programmed selling tool for literally using any product or service to market and reaching a broad audience immediately. This is incredibly important, the email method is useful for entrancing audiences to determine sale after sale spontaneously, but it is something many entrepreneurs ignore. That means you must build connections with other people, even investors, provided you have a lead magnet.

Wondering how to plan an event or ever wondered how your inspirational authors cope with creating a big stack of spectacular pages that you read avidly? Sure, there's no top secret to their achievement, and thinking about it can feel a little bit like struggling to study pseudoscience. Depending on the type of event, the need to trace costs under a microscope can stimulate innovation that results in an event full of guests and moving components. *You begin with just a dream and a plan.* Then you transform it into an event your guests will remember for all the right motivations. Below I've turned up those steps on how to use your event plan to produce a full effect with the least possible frustrations, along with a lot of attempted and valid suggestions for organizing an event.

Plan Ahead

If you don't want any traumatic encounters, organizing a productive event starts by realizing that attendees are looking for more than an event. The initial approach in throwing a more successful event includes logistics, content, and advertising. Once you have the content, design a file accessible to the whole team. You must concentrate on generating persuasive content that creates enthusiasm and draws a crowd, so each member will be able to see the responsibilities of the others and the big picture in the file. Just as concision is the mother of humor, organizing is to successful event planning, so every small detail of the event needs to map back to the objective, from the venue to the food. Deciding that the goal for the event starts by working with major stakeholders to achieve success with the main event management organizing measures. As a result, the organizing process leads to exclusive management to figure out why the event needs to take place.

Location is Everything
Location is key to hosting a top-notch event, so make sure there are enough signs all around the venue and think about what amenities will be required. Get an adaptable room that can expand or contract depending on your turnout, and it's good to have at least a few individuals who are solely in charge of directing guests go through around your venue without getting lost. Think about the focus of your event, this is your opportunity to make a great first impression instead of beginning off on the wrong foot.

Accommodate your performers/speakers
You must think about who you are planning to entice and what they'd find exciting, so the first step to appeal to speakers is to find a theme based on what your audience is attracted to. If your event depends on any speakers, it will be much easier to invite speakers once you have a specific theme in mind because it helps them envision their role in your event.

Your presenters aren't at your event to do a job, don't pay them for their presence, they're there to connect with your guests. The benefit should be mutual. Make sure you have people taking care of welcoming them and taking care of their needs—Reserve seats and possibly hotel rooms for your speakers. If you haven't met them in person before, make sure to introduce yourself. Overall, you want to demonstrate your appreciation, give them as much significance for being a part of your event as you get from having them speak, and make yourself accessible in case they have any questions or advice during the event.

Conclusion
When you consider events, you know that not everything runs to plan, and you must face countless tasks. If you've ever planned an event,

event preparation is a huge undertaking, and this rule proclaims that on the outside, you should look peaceful and determined. Whether planning a small meeting or organizing a large seminar, you might think that your business isn't big enough to hold a summit large enough to make a difference. Events, when done right, are a positive method for marketing, and there are a few components you should start to consider early on to make the procedure as stress-free as possible. No matter how easy or complicated, every event has variable goals, budgets, and audiences. It also requires detailed planning and organization.

NOTES

Overcome Business Obstacles
Passion Leads the Way
Embrace the Journey | Be Fearless
Brainstorm | Understand Finance
Nompumelelo Real Kunene
Nompumelelo Real Kunene
www.swaticanadianinternational.ca

Chapter 4

OVERCOME BUSINESS OBSTACLES

The universe can be a dull place with its challenges, mainly if you are stuck at a 9-to-5 desk job. Self-employment can be a challenging gig, and the going can get even somewhat tricky since it's up to you how, when, and where you choose to work. It can be tempting to slow down because what transpires next in your life will be on your words, and entrepreneurs have indeed built a character for cracking out of the rules. It is easier than ever to earn a living doing what you love, and the feeling of success you'll gain from it is worth the investment. The most satisfying experiences of your life are working for yourself. In this unified world, you will be your own boss, and the rewards of entrepreneurship are incredibly worthwhile.

Setting up a business involves a daunting amount of tedious, administrative tasks, and you should be ready for problems on the way to success. The beginning responsibilities can turn out to be a problem. There's legal paperwork to file, especially when you've never done them. Some people enjoy the logistical process work. It is a sign of a start-up, soon they will have unanticipated success. The first piece of information I would suggest is that, do a reality check in case you think of leaving your job and go full-time on your business. Don't give up on your dream of operating your own business. You are never closer to having what you want than the day you feel like quitting your 9-5 paycheck to paycheck job. The odds are against you.

Although most people with "normal" jobs are odd about what it would be like to be their own boss, it's also not as easy as just setting out and choosing to change the world through your unique product or service.

When one thinks about being their own boss, picture this, you've spent years working on your job that hasn't been what you needed for your life, but you smile because it's almost over. Self-employment can be a fantastic move to discovering a satisfying career. Still, one of the main challenges of being your own boss is having the commitment and inspiration to make the right options when the going gets hard.

Let's face it, being your own boss has many rewards, and one of the first things that come to mind is the independence to set your own hours. Although being self-employed is hard work, but it is worth it for every sleepless night you have. Being your own boss can be the most fulfilling experiences in your life, but often, the rewards have a reverse side. The everyday routine of working for a company that you don't care about is time-consuming. Any sensible person would have to acknowledge that self-employment is likely to come with substantial trials. From my personal experience as an entrepreneur, having a good idea of approaches to guide you as you make this move could help you decide if this is a path for you.

Passion leads the way, fuel it daily
Start by questioning your desires. This maxim seems to point in the direction of using your zeal to stimulate your business. Like any flame, transforming your enthusiasm into a flourishing company may not be as daunting as you think. Still, the obligation of whether to pursue your desire or follow the money never ends. Look for ways to utilize your current strengths, and this is crucial for you to stay driven. You may find a way to turn what you love into what you do when discovering the world of business. If you do what you love, you'll always love what you do while your people skills can make it easier to round up funding for your new enterprise.

Passion must be cherished and controlled to ensure it stays ignited, so every day, before you do anything, remind yourself why you opened your small business. This may not be perfect for every single business strategy out there, but many skills, including soft skills like communication, can help. You may not think you have the appropriate training, but it's undoubtedly true for many young entrepreneurs that your leadership abilities can help you develop a great team. Your enthusiasm motivates you and everyone around you, so maybe there's reality somewhere in the middle of these extremes. You probably should follow your desire successfully; it determines why you do what you do and why your business exists.

"For as the body without the spirit is dead, so faith without works is dead also" (James 2:26 NKJV HolyBible, 2020).

Passion stimulates a tenacious determination to correct their results to picture what they genuinely need and take the essential steps to push their business towards that dream, as often as is necessary to meet their customers' needs. By formulating your concept without limitations, will often guide you to *build the most available product in the long run*. Many businesses collapse because the entrepreneur falls in love with their favorite solution, but before you take up your desire full time, look for ways to get an insider's perspective. Therefore, make sure your passion is for resolving the challenge and use implements to make developments more efficient.

Always seek passion. If you find yourself just as enthusiastic after finding an inside view, then you can transform your desire into a thrilling, flourishing new enterprise. If you have the knowledge and the commitment to see it through, you will realize you are on the right path. *There are many approaches to test out your enthusiasm from the inside*, so figure out which part of the business drives your desire and which part nicks away at it. Business accomplishment is love-driven, not money; therefore, take care of your passion while you change the world with your business.

Discovering your desire doesn't happen overnight, though some will argue that they feel more in charge vs. having someone else controlling their decisions. Security is an impression of whether you have a boss or are your own. It takes time, a lot of effort, and sometimes some trial and error. Acquiring transparency on your objective in life is one area of concentration that is profound and limitless because there is so much that needs to be done and explored. Another right way to get energized and motivated is reading books that can help motivate you to find career achievement. Starting each day with a confident mindset will make all the change, also understand that you always have the power and influence to set yourself up for better chances. Converting your hobby into a part-time or full-time business is a chance that gives you authority for your future and being engaged in this area will help you connect everything you've ever cared about, resulting in career success.

Be Patient and Embrace the Journey
When you're starting a business from the ground, organizing ahead of time helps you expect your financing requirements and organize appropriate funding. A crucial decision is whether to involve outside stakeholders to deliver the fairness required to support additional development. You can also pursue financing in the manner of small business advances or lines of credit if needed. Notwithstanding all your worries about how extremely busy you are already in life, you feel humbled at the immensity of the job ahead of you, and excited to be part of it. This area of emphasis gives your life value and reason, you feel like a novice, but you recognize you have lots of ideas to apply and can't wait to discover them.

Having a good concept won't be enough. You already have a greater grasp of the overall focus, and you just need to strengthen your understanding in that area. But when you start from your desires, you need a well-thought-out business proposal and a prepared move to improve your possibilities of getting a shareholder. It's much easier to choose the expertise you need, just like the more knowledgeable entrepreneurs who already have a recognized network of prospective investors. Think of "mompreneurs" who sell products related to kids, they work hard and devote enough time and endeavor into establishing a business that makes significant amounts of money.

Starting a small business is typically an expensive plan, so efficient credit management and tight management of overdue arrears are vital. If you want to operate your own business, making the most excellent use of your funds should be a key component in business development and evaluating new opportunities. Finding the money needed to start a new business is no easy way, and you may also want to think about boosting funding against trade liabilities. You may need to pass up encouraging prospects if pursuing them would mean starving your underlying business of vital financing, and every aspect of working investment should be thoroughly managed to increase your free cash flow. With fewer funds available, one of the biggest challenges that you face upon running a business is thinking about how to fund the venture.

The typical entrepreneur works exceptionally long hours. This is perhaps the most traumatic task on this list. Believe it or not, you need to learn to delegate appropriately. To expand your business, have confidence in your management team and providing a day-to-day power of every aspect by assigning each team member. Whether you're just starting to discover your genuine desire or are in the middle of this journey, there's a brutal sphere that you must try to prevent as much as possible. This is one of the significant hurdles that you can face, which can lead to exhaustion and promote harmful lifestyle options. New entrepreneurs are compelled to make hundreds of choices a day.

OVERCOME BUSINESS OBSTACLES

Brainstorm
Don't be afraid to substitute what isn't working, occasionally marketing networks that appeared full of possibility don't pan out, so discovering a solution to a challenge is the first step in developing a successful business. Disappointments are an essential part of business development and new merchandise doesn't catch on as predicted. First you become mindful that something went wrong and then redirect funds appropriately and learn from those missteps. For this reason, consider re-examining your position to realize where mistakes happen, then start to figure out why.

Develop emotional rollercoaster resilience
With all challenges come frustration, your company ethos is influenced by everyone engaged with your organization. To do this well, most successful people have always discovered methods to turn their disappointments into accomplishments by letting their company morals guide all their judgments. As you expand and more people come into your company's circle, it becomes harder to exercise power over your culture and you run the possibility of having it ruined. With supporters on your side at all levels of the business, constructing a strategy that resolves difficulties and using it to your advantage can only make you productive.

Get Organized

There is only one true thing to encourage you further and help you to remain on top of things to be done - being organized. To be productive in business, you need to be organized, and it takes a certain kind of mind to think "outside the box" in the circumstances to understand the importance of a new situation. The organization will help your complete tasks and makes you believe in your purpose. You may need to spend money on staff training to ensure that your small company is delivering service better to that of your rivals. A winning entrepreneur generates the most value by analyzing their existing customer service and make the adjustments that need to be made, which is the foundation of success.

Keep Detailed Records

While you shouldn't look to please everyone all the time, nowadays, we together build an incredible service through entrepreneurship. Thus, you should concentrate your thoughts on positivity. All successful businesses keep comprehensive documents, and an excellent way to do this is to build a to-do list each day. When it comes to business, you'll know where you stand economically and what possible challenges you might be confronting as you finish each item. As expressed, by maintaining thorough records will ensure that you're accomplishing all the duties that are crucial to the survival of your business.

Be fearless and authentic

To be successful in a business mission is deemed such a formidable achievement by society. While there are obvious obstacles to face, you can't be fearful to research and learn from your competitors. Competition breeds the best outcomes; one of the biggest challenges is in defeating the fear of bouncing into a business in the first place. You need to discover how to manage your worries, just understanding this gives you time to establish approaches to conquer those challenges. If you want to set yourself apart from the crowd, your key should be a method of endless invention.

> *"The thing you fear most has no power. Your fear of it is what has the power. Facing the truth really will set you free"* (Oprah Winfrey, 2012).

Grow as a Leader

The lead-up to operating a business is a challenging commitment, once you harness your worries and be open to new approaches to your business, know that your work has just begun. Understand that you don't know everything, and you must put in more time than you would if you were working for someone else. Remain focused on accomplishing your short-term objectives, just because you open a business doesn't mean you're going to start making money instantly. Although entrepreneurship can be lonely, your greatest success will have a lot to do with how you support others to find their own. Nobody will ever understand just how much push you to put in daily, so you must learn how to be a leader on some kind of degree to encourage others to connect with you in your mission. In general, it takes time to let people know who you are, so believe in what you stand for because you've already started the journey of becoming a leader.

You'll discover beliefs about us as human beings that many of us think about great concepts but never try hard enough to accomplish. You'll hear about beliefs and choices that we all wish we could aspire to but often fail to recognize. However, this is only the starting point for those who want to be extremely useful in business. Conquering your fears and getting started is virtuous. Still, the real tests of a courageous entrepreneur will be relentless, from starting a conversation at a networking mixer, and possibly asking for the sale on a major deal. One who can fail miserably and not be afraid to brush themselves off and try over and over until they are successful is courageous.

Understand finance and risks involved

The key to being productive is taking calculated risks to help your business flourish, and that doesn't necessarily mean you need to have a lot of it when you're just getting started. If you are genuinely enthusiastic about entrepreneurship, knowing how finance works and how to use your money to grow, is the smartest way. The problem with the digital age that we live in is that most people desire all day about starting a lucrative business at the same time seeing the clock tick at their everyday jobs. The truth about the most successful business endeavors is that you will need money and knowledge, which will allow you to take all sorts of calculated consequences that can produce enormous benefits.

Business Reviews

In the time of smartphones, online evaluations have formed a new field in marketing and communication where customers perform more research than ever before choosing where to buy goods and services. Reviews are crucial for your business. Most consumers will look on search engines like Google or even on Facebook when deciding what to buy. It is easy to believe the significance of customer reviews, that links the gap between traditional word-of-mouth and a viral type of response that can sway consumer's opinion. Most entrepreneurs are mindful that positive online evaluations are good for business, but nothing emphasizes more than information, just how reviews are used and how they influence business. Customers turn to review sites to make judgments about the products and services they purchase. More than 80% of customers rely on online evaluations as much as they listen to personal suggestions.

Today's consumers are gradually trusting in reviews to gain a better knowledge of a business, so the more favorable evaluations you have, the better. Statistics examine how customers behave before and after using services or buying products, and customer feedback can undoubtedly help feed the content machine, maintaining your brand favored by systems. Online websites all have their distinctive ways of indexing and growing content, which can help build strategies to enhance business. In a world where almost, everything can be found online now, constructing up reviews of your business is the best approach to offer third-party confirmation that your company does what it says it does. These constructive reviews will help introduce confidence within your business.

NOTES

Secrets to Improve Achieve and
maintain Work-Life Balance
Prioritize Your Time and Health
Don't be Afraid to Unplug | Establish Boundaries
Reach out | Manage your Mind | Take Time Off
Creating a HARMONIOUS Work-Life Integration is CRITICAL
RISE TO GREATER HEIGHTS
Nompumelelo Real Kunene
Nompumelelo Real Kunene
www.swaticanadianinternational.ca

Chapter 5

SECRETS TO IMPROVE, ACHIEVE AND MAINTAIN WORK-LIFE BALANCE

Work weeks are when most of us tend to be the busiest and tension between work and family life is one of the most typical causes of anxiety for working adults. Often, stabilizing work and family is a problem for almost every family and balancing work/life is only achieved when you're on your own. In this efficiency-focused culture that we are living in, work takes priority over everything else in our lifetime. There are some approaches, however, for accomplishing and sustaining a healthy work/life balance that can help families survive.

Prioritize Your Time
With so many pressures on our time, you may have a to-do list with more tasks on it, but you need to set doable targets that you are enthusiastic about. As there are only 24 hours in a day, your time is too valuable to spend on pointless activities, so be considerate when you are most fruitful at work and block that time off for your most valuable work-related activities. Do a short evaluation of your regular activities, organizing your day can improve efficiency at work. At the end of every day, it's challenging to be available to everyone, so you may have to think about your principles and set some priorities centered on those standards.

You may be running several responsibilities and targets in your life, think about what tasks are most essential for attaining a healthy work-life balance and set work hours for yourself, then do everything in your ability to stick to them. Establish a timeline of your events and make your workday as constructive as possible by executing time-management approaches, which can result in more free time to relax outside of work. As a result, break down each task into elements by examining your to-do list and slashing out tasks that have little to no benefit, regarding your career, health, and relationships.

Don't be afraid to Unplug
Learn how to let go of things by building boundaries between family and work. We must establish boundaries of security between your work and family, which will give you room for other views and ideas to arise. Attempting to be everything to everyone only guarantees disappointment but having boundaries with the outside world from time to time lets us recuperate from weekly tension. Limits hold the line to protect your work from the disruption of family, using that time to relax is crucial to success because it will help you feel more motivated when you're on the clock.

Disconnecting can mean something simple, like practicing to say no when you're asked to do something extra by your boss. Cut out the things in your life that are stressing you out, as well as protect your family connection from the commitments at work. This means deciding which measures are appropriate and it'll free you up for more valuable things. With clear boundaries, the stress lifted will likely be more substantial than you had realized, and it would be easier for you to tell when your action is not in favor of one aspect of your life.

"When life seems hard, the courageous do not lie down and accept defeat; instead, they are all the more determined to struggle for a better future" (Queen Elizabeth II, 2018).

There is no 'perfect' Work-Life Balance

The order to put work away for the day seems okay. While this may seem ideal, it is not always viable. What I'm saying is, don't try to have the perfect agenda and don't put extra weight on yourself when you don't need to – at work or home. Strive for a practical one. It doesn't matter if your home's not spotlessly clean, because balance is accomplished over time, not each day. Some days, you might concentrate more on work, while other days you may have more time and strength to follow your hobbies or spend time with your loved ones. You may want to leave work early to spend your quality time with friends and family. Then you realize you haven't done something as well as you could. Letting yourself stay free to redirecting and reviewing your needs on any day is essential in finding balance. Thus, you'll have to let that go because the option to take on more work when you're already strained out can affect you. It is critical to remain flexible and continually evaluate where you are. If you're overburdened, you need to explicitly tell yourself that what you've finished may not be great, but it is good enough.

Establish boundaries for work

Accomplishing work-family life balance is a lengthy and often intimidating process, so set limits for yourself to prevent breakdown. Sit down with your boss and talk about what are the expectations for you at work and set boundaries by making sensible choices on the most critical matters in your life. I have discovered through my experience that if you do not make the deliberate decision to accomplish balance, it is likely that you will fail along the way because you are not clear on what you expect yourself to achieve. It is essential to try to give yourself a chance for balance, so when you leave the office, stop thinking about upcoming projects. For this reason, it is crucial to find yourself a job that is challenging but not suffocating, so that you can control when you will work and when you will stop working.

Flexible workplace and imbalance

With my battle to achieve an ideal balance between work and family, I've learned that those who do sustain a positive balance between work and family have often pointed to their flexible work schedules. Many employers have granted workers more flexibility both with their timetable and where they work, and I recognized that there will always be priority times for work or family. Business owners still struggle with fewer resources for benefits that cost the company, and it would always be challenging to stabilize everything in your life completely.

The problem of balancing family and work has no easy answer. Still, in the long run, employers must find approaches to extend flexible work opportunities if they want to appeal and maintain top talent. There is no one-size-fits-all method. Employers must make it the focus to give employees admission to a broader range of benefits, because stability is a very personal thing, and only you can choose the lifestyle that fits you.

Work-life balance will represent various ideas to different people because, after all, every person and family must find specific results to their concerns depending on their inclinations and desires. There is nothing immoral with working hard to improve some of the bigger things in life because we all have different life commitments that suit our specific needs to advance our health and well-being.

Reach out to your support system

I used to assume that I was the only one who could solve my work versus family life problem, but now I know that we are more fruitful and better off in our lives when we have a robust support system around us. Learn to recognize that at times the pressures upon you are more significant than what you can carry, so make it a point to habitually discuss with your loved ones their opinions and even concerns with your work. You need to create incredible support, this will open your eyes to a lot of things, but always make sure that when the wave rolls, you're ready to pick up the slack for those in your support structure. Overall, we all have challenging demands in life; make sure that the whole support system is aware of your commitments and obligations at work.

Prioritize your health and manage your mind
Whether you are a CEO or just a go-getter at work, your overall physical, emotional, and mental health should be your primary concern. It's easy to let things like exercise and diet go by the roadside once things get busy in the office, but that's the only body you're going to get, and it needs to take you until the end of the life's journey. When fear sneaks in, and you think rehabilitation would help you, fit those sessions into your schedule. If you struggle with depression, spend time with someone who will motivate your spirit and support you, perhaps do some work on your mental health such as meditation. Focusing on your health is a priority that will make you a better person; that's why it's essential to continue to keep your body strong and healthy enough. Prioritizing your health doesn't have to involve drastic activities, the point here is to be healthy enough that you don't have to say "no" to anything you want to do.

Take time off and be selfish about your "Me" time
Self-care is essential. It's something you should do, no matter how exhausted you are. Attaining work-life balance needs intentional action; you can't be the best version of yourself if you're run low and don't get a moment to rejuvenate. While your job is essential, taking a

moment to connect with yourself must be a priority. When personal matters happen, don't give up the time that you have devoted to yourself. Even when you hit a hard patch, and your calendar seems impossible, then you will eventually have to be the one in control of your time and life. No matter how chaotic your schedule might be, don't do it if you don't make time for your own private life. Push yourself out the door to the workout class you like. You will never have time to do other things outside of work. Just because your job keeps you busy doesn't mean you should abandon personal relationships, don't be tempted to ignore it when your calendar begins to get full. Irrespective of what you decide to do with your "me" time. Afterward, you will be in better health and pleased that you did something for yourself.

Take a vacation and have fun
Truly disconnecting means shutting work off for a while, even a long weekend once in four months is better than doing nothing. Keep in mind that work is only one part of you, so make time for a vacation and reserve in breaks, at least twice a year. We only go around once, whether your retreat involves a one-day staycation or a two-week trip to the Maldives, it's significant to appreciate your life and set time for fun. There is no decency in not taking a well-deserved moment away from work. It's crucial to take time off to physically and emotionally rejuvenate. With proper planning, taking holiday time will give you the chance to enjoy life both at home and work without fretting about inconveniencing your contending with a tremendous amount of work when you go back.

Finances
Whether you work for yourself or not, you'll have to be on a path to accumulate enough wealth that you will be able to enjoy a comfortable retirement. It's important to feel confident about your

finances and see if your assets are increasing over time. Cash flow is one of the biggest challenges facing small businesses, so the key to personal financial health is to feel in control.

> *"Beloved, I pray that you may prosper in all things and be in health, just as your soul prospers"* (III John 1:2 NKJV HolyBible, 2020).

Spiritual

It takes a lot of ritual to a balanced life on your spiritual side. Our personal/work life is essential to lead a satisfying experience, and our spiritual area of life needs to be cultivated too to accomplish balance and find higher value in life. This could be taking a trip to church on Sunday for your connection with God to feel restored and equipped to challenge the world. Being present is a routine, maybe you feel called to bring a change in the world, or anything that can silence the mind from unnecessary conversation can only help our productivity and focus!

NOTES

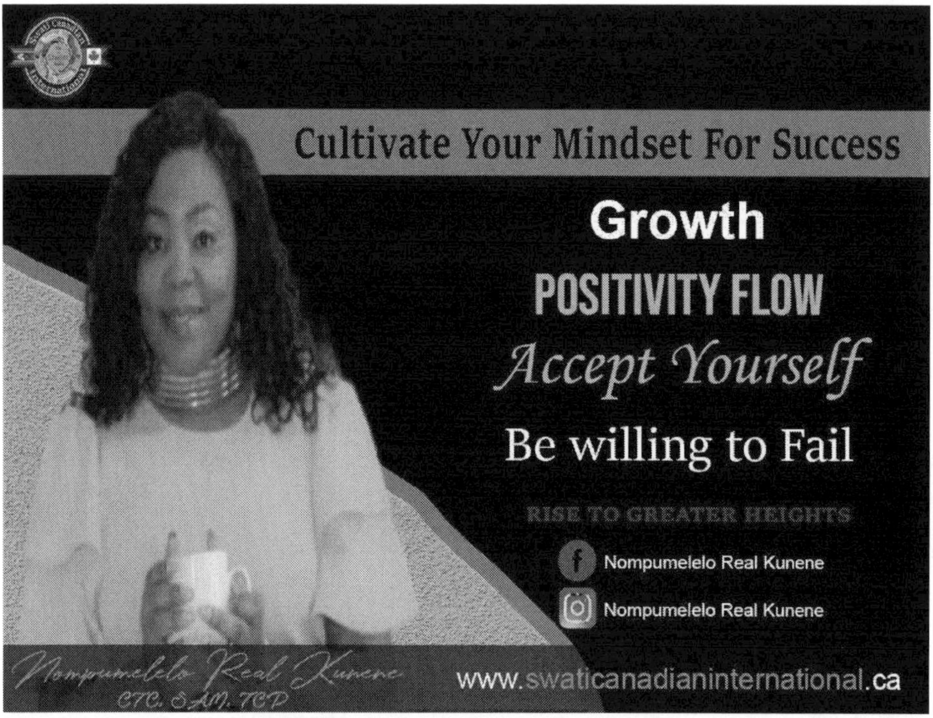
Cultivate Your Mindset For Success
Growth
POSITIVITY FLOW
Accept Yourself
Be willing to Fail
RISE TO GREATER HEIGHTS
Nompumelelo Real Kunene
Nompumelelo Real Kunene
Nompumelelo Real Kunene
www.swaticanadianinternational.ca

Chapter 6

CULTIVATE YOUR MINDSET FOR SUCCESS

Many of us tell ourselves that it's too late to change careers, perhaps you are probably like me and have many goals you want to achieve. It's impossible to change your mindset without a proper mindset. You may find yourself distracted by shiny object syndrome. Shiny object syndrome is when you are always disturbed by the most original and ultimate idea yet living with these controlling attitudes creates a self-fulfilling insight that makes us believe that we can't do anything. Whether these goals are for business or you don't have enough time to learn something new, you need to change your life. For this reason, cultivate your mindset for success with these hacks to ensure that you envision opportunities as an alternative to concentrating on barriers.

Growth
The most critical thing you can do is to adopt a growth mentality that can help you to create transformation if you work hard and execute tactics for personal development. Let's say you feel like you're always behind with everything at work. This is the approach that will push you to dream big and drive the limitations of your views to new heights. A progressive mindset says you can do it; thus, successful people are happy to keep striving until they get what they want. A fixed mindset means that the situation is the way it is, and it will never change no matter what you do, but with a growth mindset, you will be eager to try all sorts of approaches and skills because you know that you will ultimately get where you want to go.

A fixed mindset is dangerous because it will eventually suppress your capability to reach new accomplishments. In contrast, with a growth mindset, people have confidence in their gifts and abilities that can be utilized over time through understanding and mentorship. A growth mindset develops from the belief that accomplishing success is about steady progress, so instead of judging capabilities in terms of disappointments and achievements, you constructively frame them. You will have problems and difficulties along the way, but if you trust in your ability to conquer greatness, then you'll encounter that everything in your life will fall into the right path. If you pay attention to growth, understand that it can help you develop and become a better person to see accomplishment as a ride rather than a final goal. As a result, anyone can change their approach, and this means you're always open to discovering new things and developing yourself until you reach your goals.

Positivity flow
If your opinions about yourself and your capability to reach your goals are discouraging, your eagerness and positivity fade, this will let negative ideas to take control. Your values impact your outer performances and measures, so when you implement a glass-half-full attitude, it will begin to steer everything you do. Your mindset will indicate every knowledge you feed it, meaning you must have faith that you can prosper before you even try to do something. When you have a solid mindset, you need to succeed, you'll undoubtedly direct your attention toward results rather than challenges, that's why it's essential to fill your mind with useful information daily.

"Sometimes when you're in a dark place you think you've been buried, but you've actually been planted" (Christine Caine, 2016).

Even if you try to achieve your goal, the reality is that accomplishment doesn't spontaneously bring contentment, but you must have the drive and strength to manage your regular activities. It's logically recognized that optimists are more satisfied and productive than cynics because they can take further measures that are consistent with their constructive inner values, even if the path to victory is very steep and challenging to climb. An optimistic form of mind will invite success into your life; all it takes is a few easy twists to your rational to become your most satisfied self.

Accept Yourself
Positive people know who they are, and they know their strengths and weaknesses. Difficult times are par for the path for those who have great ideas, but if you keep pushing yourself down, there is no way for you to move forward. Successful people know the right attitude you can have is self-recognition because they understand how the world works, and they don't try to be incredible at everything. They know that without difficult times and disappointments, there is no knowledge and development, so they *acknowledge* themselves for who they are and work with what they are given. As mentioned, successful people refuse to be in an adversarial connection with themselves because they know there's a distinction between suffering and striving.

Although nothing worth accomplishing comes without a fight, successful people know their desires inside out, and very clear about their flaws. High go-getters never ignore that their mindset is what helps them accomplish continuing success and believe that this route will bring them the most pleasure and satisfaction. Successful people strive and feel pain, but they endure the pain because they know that when they try to change their mindset, all their other remarkable character traits come together to push them further. Therefore, they know their values because they are living their lives following goals that are on the same track with who they are, and what they consider to be their objective.

Finish what you've started

Successful people have all they need to reach their potential goals, instead of passively hoping for the best—refusing to leave things to last-minute shows inner intensity. They know and acknowledge that they can't control what the world tosses in their direction, but they have the power to make things happen. You always have an option; extraordinary events happen when you choose to take control of what you can manage and let go of the rest. Tremendously successful people are very cautious about deciding what tasks to work on, at the same time, they know that even though they are handling their ship, they can only monitor themselves. You won't see substantial progressive efforts in your life and business if you never finish what you start. Thus, successful people know that if they keep pushing further, they will ultimately reach their target. For this reason, their focus is to pursue through and complete what they started because they know that they can believe and act before the world acts upon them.

Be Willing to Fail

The number one reason some entrepreneurs don't achieve their goals, is that challenges grow in force and continually pull them down, throwing them on deviations they can't travel because they're scared to fail. If your mindset is pessimistic, fear can keep you from beginning something in the first place. With a positive mindset you will think of difficulties as a motivation to be innovative and see failure as the chance to start all over again. Successful people know that part of taking risks is being able to discover something new from your missteps, and they don't consider it as a dilemma unless it begins to become a routine. In general, when you concentrate on opportunities you have more prospects because you can use your mistake as a jumping-off point toward something new.

Continually learning

If you want to go far, you should never stop learning. The most successful people are smart decision-makers, and they stay teachable to take advantage of all life lessons. A desire for knowledge is something that can never be quenched. That means you don't pretend to know it all but are free to learning and growth. No matter what your level of education, having a constant amount of inquisitiveness is essential to seeing ahead of what's in front of you.

"Set your mind on things above, not on things on the earth" Colossians 3:2 NKJV HolyBible, 2020).

Conclusion

Once you've executed one or more of the above success practices, you will achieve your goals more productive, and you will then find yourself with the opportunity to establish new and perhaps bigger goals. If you set your mindset for success, you will draw optimistic power that helps to build a relaxed and peaceful atmosphere for you and everyone around you. A positive mindset allows you to decide how you want to live and what you want to accomplish, so keeping a consistent attitude can go a long way towards helping you stay on the road to success.

Being conscious of your mindset makes you oversee your life and keeping your head in the right place along the way is also extremely valuable. Your mindset is very influential, and each new day comes out with its new battles, but your approach has a considerable impression on how well you deal with them. Thus, your positive mindset is as vital as your best plan. It will make you feel better about yourself and help keep you on the path to success.

NOTES

Maintain a Solid
Mental health
Overcome | Know the Facts | Radical Acceptance
Speak Out | Social Connection
Nompumelelo Real Kunene
RISE TO GREATER HEIGHTS
Nompumelelo Real Kunene
Nompumelelo Real Kunene
www.swaticanadianinternational.ca

Chapter 7

SOLID MENTAL HEALTH

Mental health resides in all of us, which is a position of welfare whereby we recognize our ability, just like physical health. Mental health discloses that individuals can survive with the usual pressures of life, but unemployment is a well-documented risk influence for mental health complications. Views of humiliation by therapy providers are known to avoid people from looking for care, which leads them not to work efficiently and productively to make an impact on her or his people. A depressing working atmosphere may lead to real mental health crises since workplace shame impacts someone to quit their work. Therefore, mental health can range from good to bad, and it starts the moment you are born and endures throughout life.

Employers have a chance to control amounts of absenteeism, improve efficiency and value from related profitable benefits by endorsing a mentally healthy workplace. Environments that stimulate mental wellbeing and help individuals with psychological illnesses are more prone to lessen non-attendance, and they can make lots of changes to enhance the safety of its workers and support improved mental health. The stigma has economic damage for businesses and other struggles, which are not mental conditions, but which may be aggravated by work, such as trauma and fatigue. There are many risk factors for mental health that may be present in the working environment, and these factors can lead to physical and psychological wellbeing complications that will most likely prolong current challenges. Work is considered suitable for health; therefore, employers must be able to establish action strategies for enhancing both employee wellness and the ultimate outcome.

Consequences may also be connected to an employment position. Employers are perceived to be less helpful to staff undergoing cerebral health-associated challenges, such as giving incompatible duties for the person's abilities or a high and relentless amount of work. Experiences of discrimination and bullying are common causes of work-related stress preventing employees from revealing a mental challenge to their co-workers. Some jobs may involve an elevated personal danger than others, which can have costs for businesses in terms of decreased efficiency and increased employee turnover. As expressed, most possibilities correlate to connections between type of work, which can influence mental health and be a source of signs of mental illnesses.

We can make a difference through appropriate steps; mental health management programs in the workplace can have a valuable benefit from the employer's view. An imperative component of reaching a healthy workplace is the progress of administrative regulation, and employees with mental health illnesses can be just as valuable as other employees if they have the right to all the support within the organization. Therefore, enhancing mental health at a very early stage in life will lessen imbalances because a healthy workplace can be portrayed as one where employees and leaders aggressively contribute to the working environment.

Schools are an excellent place for kids to be taught about mental well-being, so establishing protective components, such as self-esteem, stress handling abilities, and feelings of mastery, teachers can work to raise awareness with their students. Inspiring students to be engaged in the opportunities at school can help overall mental health, this will help stabilize discouraging influences in the lives of children and youth. Executing and aggressively endorsing strategies for accommodating schools, recognizing students in danger, and assisting them to get the help they need are all responsibilities that the education approach can play. To be most effective, fostering positive mental health, including bullying prevention and mediation programs, can be part of an entire school method, delivering education to children, youth, and their families. For this reason, schools and communities are the ideal settings to stimulate mental health by stressing the point that mental health is an essential part of life and the notion of improvement from mental illness.

Students should be healthy, and to better meet the demands of those served and to serve more significant numbers, school-based mental health benefits must be offered to many students who need support. Evolving trends are pressing for reforming of school-owned programs so that they can fully engage in school and community activities. Because wellbeing is not the primary business of schools, priority must be given to challenges outlined in legislative obligations. And because funds are scarce, a school's reaction to mental health and psychosocial matters typically is limited to targeted complications seen as immediate obstacles to learning. Overall, students spend most of their lives at school, so fostering positive mental health in schools is a joint assignment of parents and educators.

Understanding mental health must be an essential topic for all educators, since mentally healthy students tend to be more effective in school and life general. Education professionals must recognize the influence that a student's psychological wellbeing has on understanding and accomplishment, and there should be an enduring significance of advocating the positive mental welfare of children and young people. Grappling with a mental health problem can affect students' school life, so educators who are often the first line of protection for their students must understand that there's a fantastic strategy that can be taken to help students with mental health issues. As a result, mental health awareness must be a crucial part of a school's syllabus, and this will be done through influencing or recognizing brain growth and efficient educational curriculums.

There are several distinct ways that schools can do to help the emotional wellness and educational development of all students. Some of these services are beyond the school procedure, such as evaluating mental health demands through comprehensive, selective, and targeted mediations or transferral to a therapist. Other benefits are available in the school system itself, such as admission to social and mental wellness services or visiting an in-school counselor. Services and supports may be different from each school, and it can be accessed by forming collaborative connections between the school, students' families, and communities. Key components to spark a light on incorporating the concept of personal-care for one's mental health is leveraging higher-intensity personnel for essential assistance and services. Until mental health training is compulsory in all schools, working together and communicating this unique knowledge can help to build an effective plan. Everyone in the community has a responsibility in creating the most suitable support strategy, so combining broad services and assistance throughout every grade level can improve academic confidence and commitment in education and community life.

Overcoming
Mental illness is almost everywhere than most people have imagined. While resources like medication and psychotherapy are incredibly helpful, sometimes people undergoing mental health challenges face discrimination in such a way that someone will make a negative comment about their mental illness or their treatment. Everyone can

experience mental illness at any point in life, but the stigma of the belief that you'll never be successful at trials or that you can't change your condition can be very harmful. Anyone can suffer from emotional health difficulties, yet, despite how typical mental condition crises are, many of us do not attempt to develop our condition. The shame and confusion of mental illness in society prevent patients from asking for help and getting treatment. Sometimes it may be inadvertent, in such a way that most people will avoid you because they believe that you are unstable due to your cerebral illness.

Don't let stigma build uncertainty and embarrassment about your wellness, find a reason, and value in life. Everyone achieves goals in various ways that include helping others, so having robust mental health doesn't mean that you never go through awkward moments or encounter disturbing situations. Humiliation doesn't just come from those around you, sometimes you may falsely believe that your condition is an indication of personal vulnerability, and this leads to stigma. People who are emotionally and psychologically strong have the means for surviving every challenging circumstance, but at times seeking counseling about your situation can help you surmount damaging acumen. We all go through setbacks that can trigger nervousness and tension in our lives. Still, discovering value is necessary to improve our immune system and help us to be determined to follow measures to improve mental and emotional wellness.

> *"It's time to tell everyone who's dealing with a mental-health issue that they're not alone, and that getting support and treatment isn't a sign of weakness—it's a sign of strength"* (Michelle Obama, 2015).

We need to raise our voices to fight against stigma related to mental illness, with the hope that it will help lessen self-stigma someone with a mental disorder may feel. New improvements are being made in mental health therapy, and I think that stigma teaching needs to be continuing instead of a one-time thing, and if possible, it needs to tackle many stigmas all at once. Education is vital, and it's good to be mindful of helpful, accurate information concerning mental illness. Still, there are other things you can do to help ease the stigma associated with mental illness. Every day, in every possible way, we need to recognize that mental disability paves the way for evidence-based therapies and treatment options. Hence, we need to erase the stigma.

Know the facts and educate yourself
Whether you're fighting emotionally, or you know someone who is, acquire knowledge about mental disorder including substance use conditions. Being knowledgeable is one of the best approaches to fight stigma, so take every opportunity to get information or share own battles with mental sickness. Focus on the positive; that means owning your life and refusing to let others determine how you see yourself. Mental disability is only part of anyone's bigger picture, so combat stigma by deciding to live an inspired life.

"casting all your care upon Him, for He cares for you" I Peter 5:7 NKJV HolyBible, 2020).

Radical Acceptance
You don't have any control over the reality that you have a mental disorder, but remember that emotional health illnesses are curable, so there's no need to fight in silence. Don't let the anxiety of being considered mentally disturbed stop you from getting help, because any time you spend in denial is only consuming you of valuable strength. You may be hesitant to acknowledge that you need

86

treatment; in fact, untreated mental disorders can often have dangerous effects. Therapy can provide relief by identifying what's wrong and reducing symptoms that interfere with your work and personal life, so it's crucial to seek help from a counselor. Therefore, accept your illness then take the essential measures to take care of yourself, because rehabilitation can give you a safe place to share your worries about stigma or how people will view you.

Speak out against Stigma
A considerable part of your healing is coming to grips with who you are, so don't detach yourself from your loved ones, but instead, think about voicing your feelings to them. Reach out to people you trust for the kindness, provision, and sympathy you need. It can help instill bravery in others facing similar situations; therefore, assess your negative thinking to understand that you aren't your illness and be mindful of your feelings and conduct.

Social Connection
It doesn't matter how much time you dedicate to developing your mental and emotional health, talking to someone can swiftly put the brakes on adverse anxiety reactions like "fight-or-flight." Devoting valuable time to people who matter to you, is the most efficient approach to alleviate your suffering. Phone calls and social networks have their place. However, you will still need Face-to-face social interaction with others to perform at your most productive behavior. Overall, humans are social creatures with emotional needs for relationships and constructive influences to help each other feel better even if they're unable to alter the stressful situation itself. In conclusion, reaching out is not a sign of faintness, and it won't make you a heavyweight to others.

NOTES

Increase your Emotional Intelligence
Self-Awareness
Self-Regulation
Empathy
Relationship Management
Social Awareness
Motivation
RISE TO GREATER HEIGHTS
Nompumelelo Real Kunene
Nompumelelo Real Kunene
Nompumelelo Real Kunene
www.swaticanadianinternational.ca

Chapter 8

EMOTIONAL INTELLIGENCE

If you desire to be in a leadership position, there's an emotional aspect you need to think about, which is the capability to be sensitively in harmony with yourself and your feelings. Emotional intelligence has to do with one's power to both acknowledge and manage their reactions, keeping an optimistic outlook, and supporting each other's views despite misunderstanding, even during tough times. Those with a high level of emotional intelligence has a relationship with their feelings. They also can acknowledge, connect to, and impact the emotions of others. Individuals who do exceptionally well in their emotional intelligence can be easy to understand other emotions because they know what they're experiencing and how these feelings can influence or hurt other people. As expressed, effective leaders know that they are not flawless, but they are mindful that they are more likely to thrive at taking the company further because they are easy going, strong, and positive.

The most successful leaders are all the same in one critical aspect: they are conscious of their powers and limitations and make every effort for continuous progress. Most people make blunders around emotional intelligence because they don't admit their own mistakes. They don't learn from faults and are incapable of assigning individuals or at least realizing what's going on with other people. Without contemplation, we cannot know who we are; therefore, for leaders, having emotional intelligence is especially important for achievement. To reach your full potential, you must try to be emotionally unbiased and earn the qualities that allow you to have emotional intelligence. Those that have a solid knowledge of what they want to work on can develop themselves regularly by linking to underlying feelings and being mindful of how those emotions influence your decisions and behaviors.

Emotional intelligence is universally recognized to be a significant factor of effective leadership that is consequently an essential trait for anyone at any level of an organization. Emotional intelligence is especially critical for those who hold positions of leadership in an organization because it helps everyone engaged feel encouraged and appreciated by the leader. As an entrepreneur, I have faced many emotions and become very mindful of the sensitivity towards others' feelings, while controlling said emotions properly to have an ideal outcome as circumstances influence.

"A fool vent all his feelings, But a wise man holds them back" (Proverbs 29:11 NKJV HolyBible, 2020).

For leaders, having emotional intelligence is vital to understand other people on what inspires them and how to work together with them. No matter what leaders set out to do, they need to shout out at their team when under pressure or remain in power because their success depends on how they handle every challenge. People with a high degree of emotional intelligence are self-aware and know how their verbal and non-verbal interactions can affect the team. Mastering leadership of self-entails acknowledging you're not perfect but trying for advancement to recognize and handle your own emotions, as well as understand and impact the feelings of those around you. Therefore, having the capability to keep calm, deal well with tension, and remaining confident often leads to improved business results, happier employees, and more productive teams.

Whether it's establishing a plan or organizing teams to action, emotional intelligence on workplace performance is an enormous benefit in developing an extraordinary team. The absence of emotional intelligence within the senior team is one of the most common reasons that lead to preservation concerns, which can threaten the working relationships with employees. A leader who is deficient in emotional intelligence is not able to successfully measure the desires of those they manage. As much as they can distort and hide their feelings, they must deal with their emotions along the way because they can never eradicate them. Leaders who fail in this primeval undertaking of guiding their feelings in the right way can generate uncertainty amongst their staff. If leaders react from their situations without assessing them, nothing they do will work as well as it could.

A leader's emotional intelligence can have a broad impact over their connections, and it can comprise of these five attributes: self-recognition, self-management, compassion and relationship management, social awareness, and inspiration.

Self-Recognition
Self-recognition is the capability to understand your feelings as they happen to manage them better. It relates to understanding one's feelings and attitudes, also having a clear image of your strengths and flaws. Being self-aware when you're in a management role means that you know how you feel and what your powers and boundaries are, at the same time, behaving with humbleness. Internal awareness isn't eradicating feelings from choices, but to understand your emotions and the impact they have on you and your team's accomplishment. It describes your capability not only to recognize your strengths and faults but instead letting them work with prudence, so they don't suppress decisions. Frequently, making sound judgments needs an

insight into how your emotions are influencing the decision to bring out the best in others.

The best leaders are self-aware of not only their feelings, despite their position of power still performs from an approach of humbleness. Through opinions, they earn insights into their performance and learn how they're apparent in the organization. Self-awareness is at the heart of everything. Some companies are forcing executives to concentrate on emotional intelligence as a component of their leadership training productivity. A manager who isn't a good delegator but is self-aware about that inadequacy can make a mindful exertion to assign out responsibilities more and have the confidence to the people that those duties have been given. Thus, a self-aware leader upholds a clear image of who they are, and when they encounter tough emotions, they slow down to examine why.

Self-Management
Emotional intelligence produces self-regulation that precludes the moments you wish you may swallow words you've said by mistake. This includes monitoring our unruly feelings and adapting to change situations. Self-control correlates to regulating our behaviors, and leaders who have the highest degree in controlling themselves do not make impulsive decisions or compromise their morals. It is all about staying in control, but leaders who lack self-management tend to make sensitive judgments. For this reason, you need to keep an optimistic view and instincts in check despite obstacles, especially in demanding circumstances, because leaders who make reckless choices lose the respect of their subordinates.

When you take on a leadership role, you can no longer afford to fear when situations get tense. It requires you to realize how important it is to remain dedicated to your responsibility in controlling your reactions and how they impact others. It's crucial to learn to take a breather, gather yourself together, and do whatever it takes to handle your feelings because when you stay calm and optimistic, you can feel and connect more clearly with your team. Self-regulation helps you to be more in harmony with your emotional intelligence to avoid mistreating your opportunity of leadership to hurt others. Overall, you need to enhance your capability of self-control by taking a minute to reflect on your emotions. It's essential to make a dedication to confess to your faults and to cope with the effects, instead of acting irresponsibly.

Compassion and relationship management
Compassion is what lets you put yourself in other people's shoes and being able to understand the emotions and opinions of others without criticizing them. As a leader, this means continually challenging yourself and recognizing that there will be some difficulties along the road. Exceptional leaders almost always find approaches around the barriers and examine the emotional atmosphere in any setting where they are, which makes them good at working with and leading others.

"We are all a little broken. But last time I checked, broken crayons still color the same" (Trent Shelton, 2015).

Leaders with this understanding enthusiastically support the professional and personal development of their team members. They're beneficial in the manner they work together with people and getting other people to feel good even if the situation is a challenging one. Some choose to avoid tension, but these leaders offer criticism without humiliating the other person. They seek regular critique from their employees because it's essential to tackle matters as they occur correctly. They can walk into a room and lift people up because they believe in building and keeping valuable connections to achieve better emotional intelligence.

If you want to keep your team happy, you need to have those challenging discussions to comprehend better what inspires or upsets them to move your team in the desired path. People with high emotional intelligence have a better awareness of their emotional conditions, which is very crucial when it comes to effectively leading an organization. Such leaders are what it takes to inspire people to perform beyond their abilities, and when one has compassion, the ability to feel empathy is accessible. For business leaders, this understanding place them in their employees' shoes, and the passion that they feel in response to pain inspires a need to help. Overall, use your new intuitions to motivate your employees and use your understanding of your feelings and the others' emotions to handle interactions effectively.

Social Awareness
While it's imperative to know and control your own emotions, leaders who do well in the social component of emotional intelligence can recognize others' feelings, and the dynamics lead them to be as open to hearing disturbing news as good news. They're experts at getting their team to support them and able to pick up on emotions in other people precisely. Leaders must know how to resolve conflicts between their team members, which comes in very handy when it comes to enabling them to communicate and collaborate more effectively with their peers, and getting their team pumped about a new project. As a result, socially conscious leaders are good at handling change and resolving disputes discreetly, which makes their subordinates confident enough to update them on anything.

Inspiration
Self-motivation correlates to internal drive that leaders show as they work consistently toward their objectives. They develop a healthy emotional relation to the outcomes they pursue from their hard work, inspire their team, and they have exceptionally high standards for the excellence of their work. In general, motivated leaders are usually confident, and they can meet a standard of excellence by acting on opportunities no matter what problems they face.

Conclusion
Emotional intelligence is an attribute that can be built to define business accomplishment. Leaders set the attitude of their organization by recognizing and controlling their emotions of those around them. If they are mindful of others' possible emotional effects, then they can organize the best possible approaches. Emotional intelligence plugs into a fundamental aspect of human behavior that can help them become better leaders in changing conditions in their workplaces. When a leader is emotionally intelligent, they can use feelings to push the organization ahead and promote safe and sound environments for employees to recommend proposals and to voice their views.

Fortunately, emotional intelligence can be enhanced to develop a cooperative performance culture in the workplace, communicate tactical concepts, and make hard decisions as a leader. By mastering emotional intelligence, you can persist in improving your profession and organization, because you will not take things personally and can forge ahead with plans without being concerned about the effect on your personality. Emotional intelligence has lately become one of the crucial talking moments that allows individuals to be more flexible in society. The benefits people and organizations can understand from emotional intelligence are unquestionable, since leaders can convey that big picture to others and guarantee achievement through motivating and by interacting. Lastly, using emotional intelligence to management is exceptionally instinctive; therefore, to improve your leadership abilities, you need to focus on the attributes mentioned above.

NOTES

LEADERSHIP
A great leader is
always able to lead a team to success
RISE TO GREATER HEIGHTS
Nompumelelo Real Kunene
Nompumelelo Real Kunene
www.swaticanadianinternational.ca

Chapter 9

EFFECTIVE LEADERSHIP

Many leaders are failing to promote a sense of trust in their employees, though to be able to cultivate crucial traits, is what makes a leader! Regardless if they have worked their way up the corporate ladder or just started their own business, leaders must have specific abilities and foster the development of certain qualities within their personality. To help them accomplish improved outcomes for their company and make them a better leader, here are the essential attributes that make a great leader.

Vision and purpose driven
Having a clear vision transforms the individual into a unique kind of person; they not only envision the future themselves but also share their idea with their supporters. Great leaders have a dream, not only does a good leader view a situation, but they are enthusiastic about their work. They are dedicated enough to accomplish constructive outcomes at any cost. Once prepared, audacity allows leaders to move up and push things in the right way so that high performance is easily characterized and scrutinized. Rather than preventing difficulties, they pursue up on all exceptional matters, create policies, and examine the efficacy of company strategies. When tested, they don't give in too quickly, but they have an exhilarating notion of where they are going and what they are attempting to achieve. Therefore, leaders should also be self-driven; such commitment is necessary since it inspires a sense of accountability in the team members to work harder in aiming to accomplish better outcomes for the company.

"No dream is too big. No challenge is too great. Nothing we want for our future is beyond our reach"
(Donald, Trump, 2017).

A good leader is usually motivated, and employees are easily attracted to them and feel more positive as a result. Focused exceptional leaders plan everything on time, this value of vision changes a transactional manager into an influential leader; because they consider the potential consequences of their decisions and determine approaches and practices that strengthen the idea. Not only are the best leaders positive, but their confidence is transmissible, as they plug into the passions of their employees. A great leader goes above and gives responsibilities to their best shot, because it will not only earn the admiration of their team members, but it will also inspire a new sense of power in them. In general, a leader's job is not limited to getting a job done, but instead, they are the guiding influence in the team and someone the team could look up to because they are full of enthusiasm and dedication.

Honesty and Integrity
The ultimate value of leadership is undeniably honesty, whether it's giving appropriate recognition for achievements or placing security and excellence first. Great leaders always demonstrate integrity, and without honesty, the organization won't achieve feasible success, so remember to lead by example. Integrity is one of the leadership traits that identify a good leader. Leaders exemplify these principles so blatantly that no employee questions their reliability for a minute. Honesty and moral values mirrored by leadership in any organization are a manifestation of yourself. If you make explicit and ethical conduct as a significant value, your team will follow. A great leader is the one who sticks with the truth and inspires their people by establishing high but achievable requirements and opportunities. Make sure your organization emphasizes the significance of honesty

to leaders at different levels to see how reasonable one can be when everyone around them is deceitful. When you are accountable for a team of people, it is essential to be honest. Thus, fairness and truthfulness are the two primary components that make a good leader. Leaders prosper when they stick to their principles and fundamental principles by doing what's right, even if that isn't the best thing for the existing plan or even the bottom line. Honesty is vital for the individual and the organization. Leaders should be particularly ethical and consider that integrity and consistency form the basis of success. Though it may not certainly be a metric in employee appraisals, honest, influential leaders treat people the way they want to be treated. Honesty is a start of opinion rather than something situational. It's mainly critical for top-level directors who are making numerous other substantial decisions. Leaders should not be able to decide when to lie and when to tell the truth, great leaders represent the principles they want to see in their teams and urge everyone to pursue in suit. The true mark of leadership operates as a model for how every employee should behave, and leeway to follow those objectives and become the best employees they can conceivably be. As expressed, integrity and trustworthiness form the basis of success. These are the most critical leadership traits that empower leaders to stand up for what they believe in.

Delegation and Empowerment

Delegating is one of the fundamental obligations of a leader; you need to concentrate on key responsibilities while leaving the rest to others. Your capability to get everyone working and pulling together is vital to your success. A good leader has confidence in their capacity to prepare and grow the employees under them. Irrespective of the condition and stance you are in, a single individual will fall short of achieving everything at once, and leaders understand this before anyone else does. They have the eagerness to encourage those they lead to acting independently. Always remember that you can't do everything on your own. Therefore, great leaders manage to delegate smaller errands to their team members while directing their focus on major tasks. Good leaders recognize that delegation does more than merely assigning the job to someone else, by encouraging their followers and delegating tasks to them. The purpose isn't just to free yourself up and increase the collaboration of others, by committing to getting along well with each key person every single day but lead to better decision-making to help your direct reports develop.

Leadership is the capability to get people to work for you because they want to and delegating to others shows that you have faith in their skills, and this can result in constructive confidence in the workplace. Your employees want to feel respected and trusted. With this, they are more likely to make decisions in the best interest of the company and the customer. When employees are encouraged, they would usually feel grateful that they got chosen, and they would feel the significance of having them around. On the other hand, leaders that continue to micromanage impede the skills of their team members, and it will create a lack of confidence, and more importantly, this conduct often leads to poor outcomes. If you continue to micromanage your subordinates, you will not be able to concentrate on significant matters, so delegate errands to your subordinates and see how they accomplish their tasks. It is confiding and trusting that your employees can manage the assignment given to them, so your capability to work well with them daily is vital to the effortless operation of the organization.

Great leaders not only inspire their employees, but they also provide them with all the resources to accomplish the goal and allow them to bear the responsibility. In this way, you exhibit a sense of trust, which helps inspires your team to work better and that your team members are totally up to any challenges they face.

Motivation

Perhaps the most challenging job for a leader is to encourage others to follow, but for the economy, great leaders inspire others to do more. Put it all together, and what develops is a picture of the genuinely motivating leader who challenges their people by setting high but attainable principles. Inspiring is a value that describes a good leader; organizations must discover the best ways to cultivate these essential qualities in current and developing leaders. Being able to motivate your team is great for concentrating on the company's concept and targets, and as a leader, you should be optimistic. This positive attitude should be evident through your measures. The best leaders are a foundation of upbeat power; they always seem to have an answer and still know what to say to motivate and restore confidence. When the going gets steep, having the quality of audacity means that you are inclined to take risks in the success of your goals with no guarantee of achievement, and your team looks up to you and see how you respond to the condition.

"Fear not, for I am with you; Be not dismayed, for I am your God. I will strengthen you, Yes, I will help you, I will uphold you with My righteous right hand" Isaiah 41:10 NKJV HolyBible, 2020).

Individuals become leaders because they are enthusiastic about their career and avoid personal condemnation but look for avenues to increase harmony and get people to work together effectively and successfully as a team. A constructive position and an honest concern for the wellbeing of their employees is yet another characteristic of great leaders because there is no assurance in life or business, every dedication you make involves a risk of some kind. All these traits are essential to excellent management because these individuals love what they do, and always know what to say to motivate and encourage the same amount of enthusiasm in other people. While a passionate attitude can never act as a replacement for other leadership qualities, it is your job to keep spirits up, and that begins with an admiration for the hard work that they have put in. If you are competent in motivating your subordinates, you can easily surmount any existing and potential challenge because you have an innovative concept and knows how to transform your ideas into real-world success stories.

Good Communicator

Good leaders always have a vision, they convey their strategies to significant players and have contingency proposals if last-minute adjustments need a new direction. Leaders must encourage and discipline the people they are in charge of, so until you communicate your vision to your team and tell them the strategy to achieve the goal, it will be tough for you to get the results you want. You need to be able to connect in a variety of methods, from communicating to training your people, if you are unable to convey your message efficiently to your team, you can never be a good leader. When a new focus is required, leaders speak openly and take accountability for everyone's performance, because they understand their concepts and policies are well-advised and the consequence of much hard work. Words have the power to push people to do the impossible, and anyone who can master it can be a great leader, thus with excellent communication, your employees will have a clear insight into what they are working for.

Efficient leadership and effective communication are interlinked, but it also essential to keep in mind that listening is an integral part of communication. It's critical to see that communication skills are not just about voicing views in the best conduct, but if you use them effectively, you can also achieve better results. You must be able to connect with a variety of people across the roles. Therefore, overcoming the fear of speaking in front of people is what makes a good leader become a great leader. A good speaker can be a good leader. The one who can successfully communicate their thoughts and vision is the one who will see constructive outcomes. Communication should be consistent when it comes to forming work expectations or giving positive feedback. Leaders must know how to make use of this ability to inspire and train their team members. As mentioned, words have the power to inspire people and make them do the impossible, so the capability to communicate well is a valued ability, not just in employees, but in leaders as well.

Decision-Making Capabilities
A good leader knows when not to act alone and is empowered to make choices due to their role, but the economy goes on to acknowledge that great leaders know their boundaries and include other opinions and views into their decision-making. Remarkable leaders don't waver in such circumstances. They are eager to take on the risk of decision making, risks that have a profound influence on the masses. As a result, great leaders know that when it comes to their company or workplace, they take risks knowing that if things don't work out, they'll need to take personal accountability for malfunction, and hold themselves responsible first and foremost.

A leader should think before deciding, rather than merely making judgments. Many leaders allow the discussion to continue and then establish a piecemeal judgment that pleases no one. Although most leaders make conclusions on their own, they know that in some circumstances, hard and appropriate decisions must be made in the best interests of the whole organization. All leaders must sometimes make difficult choices, decisions that involve influence and determination that will not please everyone. A good leader does not make justifications. After all, they are the ones who will gain or endure your decisions, so they take the responsibility irrespective and then work out how to resolve the dilemma as soon as possible.

Accountability
When it comes to responsibility, a good leader remains accountable for everyone's performance within the organization. If something goes awry, leaders take little more than their portion of the responsibility. They must be ready to hold themselves or their teams accountable without being unfair in their behavior. When things are going well, this kind of performance will make the team see their mistakes and will generate a sense of accountability among them, however, when problems arise, they seek results and get the team back on track. For this reason, make sure that every one of your underlings is responsible for what they are doing, holding them accountable for their actions will create a sense of accountability.

Empathy
Having compassion as a leader goes a long way, they guide employees through challenges, and always on the look for keys to nurturing the long-term success of the organization. Leaders should cultivate empathy with their followers; in other words, they should put themselves in other people's shoes. Great leaders applaud in public and address challenges in private, while they look for positive results and focus on moving forward. Empathy is associated with job execution, try to show more compassion towards your direct reports in your organization, and make even tension-riddled discussions an opportunity for professional growth. Then you'll be more likely to be perceived as a better player by your boss.

Creativity and Innovation

As a good leader, you must be ready to convert your innovative spirit into an invention that sets you apart from the rest, so it is up to you to think outside the box when any problems occur. The thing that separates a leader from a follower is that a leader is innovative and ground-breaking to come up with distinctive concepts and turn those ideas and ambitions into reality. You can mobilize the team and start suggesting ideas to develop upon some of your plans to get ahead in today's fast-paced world. As seen, innovative thinking and continuous improvement are what makes you and your team stand out from the crowd. This is the true quality of a leader that continually pushes you out of your safe zones.

Self-Awareness and Humility

While this is a more profoundly focused skill, leaders know that there are apparent differences between management and employees. Self-awareness is the utmost for leadership, so use this expertise to maintain a professional and objective distance for the best interests of the organization. Great leaders are those who are pivotal but also respectful, and that is why the leadership styles most great leaders embrace put lots of weight on team dynamics instead of focusing on self-promotion. A good leader is always noble and always thinks about their followers since pride won't get in the way of collecting the information; they need to accomplish the best outcomes.

Managerial competence

We often hear that many organizations try to create leaders from people who are merely good at their jobs because good workers know the company's strategies. To be clear, those who arise as being outstanding workers often have essential attributes and have a strong knowledge of what the company offers in terms of products and services.

Conclusion

To join the influential club of good leaders, you need to focus on outcomes and on what must be accomplished by you and your team. A leader is not the one who has held a dominant position in a firm. A leader must have all these traits to focus on the needs of the company and the condition. On top of this, a natural-born leader focuses on strengths and has the natural force to mentor, inspire, and guide other people to set an excellent example for others to follow. Not everyone is or can be a natural-born leader. Your capability as a leader to call the shots and make sure that everyone is focused on the most critical use of their time is the necessary traits listed above, and if applied correctly, can yield positive outcomes. You can strive to make the point in the world of leadership.

NOTES

Empowerment

10 empowerment guidelines to enable your team

Openness to New Ideas | Developing others

Trust | Constructive Feedback | Recognition

Give team authority | Stop Micromanaging

Communicate | Provide Resources

Shared Responsibility

RISE TO GREATER HEIGHTS

Nompumelelo Real Kunene
Nompumelelo Real Kunene

www.swaticanadianinternational.ca

Chapter 10

EMPOWERMENT

Team liberation is directly bound to outcomes, and most directors regularly encourage their team by giving influence and decision-making. The more you empower your employees, the more they will flourish, and it takes a leader that is enveloped by empowered staff to do this. Once you have a controlled atmosphere that enables the empowerment of the team, you'll want to drill along and make sure that each team member has specific traits that will help them support the team. If you're going to enhance your culture, keep your aptitude and expand your profits, you better start embarking on a policy to give your employees the liberty and obligation to do their job their way. Although it might sound formidable, this style of leadership works best in encouraging certain types of execution and employees.

As a small business owner, becoming a leader that your employees will appreciate and admire is feasible, and it takes a distinct kind of a leader to develop a billion-dollar company. You have the idea of where you want your business to go, all you need to do is encourage your employees to see that dream and work towards attaining it. This can be done through leadership; inspiring leaders should understand when they can be most successful by establishing a team that is eager to share your vision and take your business to the next level. Here are ten empowerment guidelines to enable your team to make decisions for your business. These ideas will undoubtedly empower your team at the workplace, which will help you to lead them efficiently.

Openness to New Ideas and Input
Micromanagement produces a culture of distrust, but if a leader is receptive and welcoming new viewpoints from team members, empowerment will be substantially better. Some decisions within a development will be more critical than others, so empowering leaders will be more efficient at motivating staff inspiration and social responsibility behavior than regular task performance. Often when employees come up with new proposals, but too many directors try to get employees to say what they want to hear. You want to prevent stipulating how every little aspect of development should be implemented; it is far wiser to pay attention cautiously for the honesty and then change your conduct in reaction to that fact. Create an atmosphere where team members are happy voicing their remarks and, when possible, include your employees in decision-making and goal setting.

To further empower the team, individuals will occasionally have exceptional opinions, so feel free to test with new proposals. Urge your team members to participate in brainstorming activities. It can open your organization to great new ideas. Overall, empower your team by delegating power to your employees and inspire independent decision-making.

Developing Others
Make mentorship a priority. Don't just be a manager, but you must offer robust methods for your employees to flourish. Be a guide to your team because these people must cultivate new abilities; therefore, ask your staff about their professional aspirations, then give strengths-based duties. If your employees never have great concepts, coach, and guide them to perform autonomously, then assist them in achieving their potential by offering training and advancement opportunities to support them get there. Enquire about progress and

ask for their visions, also provide sufficient support, and extensive training for areas workers want to enhance upon. Ask your team to be a component of the decision-making procedure and ask how you can develop your approach to be more efficient. This gives team members power, which in turn adds stimulates for more encouragement. When you delegate, you are more likely to be trusted by your subordinates, so make sure you mention the sureness you have in your team members to implement.

Model encouraging conduct yourself, a better awareness of your team helps you lead them more efficiently. This can be at work and in their personal life. If you want better performance from your team members, offer them more opportunities to sparkle by enabling them to challenge duties fit to their strengths, and by assisting them in accomplishing their ambitions, you're helping the whole team and boosting productivity. Assign projects to team members and participate in growth to help them expand their knowledge of ideas where they're missing. Have a positive mindset at work and acknowledge employees who do the same; this gives them a feeling of importance within the organization. Designate duties to high-performing team members and make them heads on specific responsibilities, high employment emancipation substantially contrasts with a positive work environment.

Trust
Empowerment can be developed if you have confidence in your team; this fosters an internal coherence among the group that not merely empowers them but makes their work more effective. The best way to increase employee allegiance is by showing your staff that they have your confidence and give them the quantity of power they need to finish the task without checking back with you on every aspect. The ability of a manager to earn respect and assistance from the team

members is another essential element. Still, you should find better approaches for people to help each other by bringing them collectively to support and inspire each other.

The best leaders get excellent performance from rational human beings who are more likely appraised by their co-workers as being extremely innovative and good managerial citizens. Demonstrate that you have confidence in your team members. If employees can rely on their manager and felt the boss would assist them, they are more likely to feel empowered. I know it may be hard to have confidence in assigning a project to a new employee in the business. Still, in gaining trust, you promote incredible loyalty and determination in your employees. Explain the ends instead of the means, your employees will never feel as though they're competent in their work if you do not trust in them yourself, so let your staff go about tasks in their way. The interdependence that is vital to encouraging the team is built on confidence; this type of leadership appears to inspire employees to generate new concepts and think of new conducts of doing things.

Empowerment involves additional attempts and strength from employees, they might not complete everything just as you would have, but they will get the job done with their talent. Trust that they are skilled enough to do their job and that each team member is not slacking off but working carefully to keep up their completion of the development. To fully inspire the team means that you must allow them to make decisions on their own, assist others in the workplace, and be eager to support their organization beyond an executive position.

The mystery to empowering teams is that while they can work independently, you are also granting them all the opportunity that they need to thrive and grow. When there is a low level of confidence in a team leader, and without the capability to perform with influence on those facets of the development that your team is an expert on is not power, it will lead to employees avoiding liberation. There is the necessity to have confidence in other members of the group, give them this opportunity to prove themselves unified in working towards a shared objective, and that they should only ask for assistance from you as a last option. If managers are successful in two-way communication and relinquish themselves from many of those approval practices to genuinely enable their team, these skills will produce better empowerment.

Recognition, rewards, and encouragement
Empowerment needs team members to make some attempt and take some risks, thus, demonstrating gratitude for work well done makes it more likely that a person will do it again. Things that are rewarded are echoed; therefore, by applauding the effort, you will inspire people to learn and flourish, this will guarantee sustained high-quality work in the future. When your employees learn new talents, it's better for the company, rather than to just stay engaged on the one thing that comes naturally to them. Sure, your employees are paid to show up every day, but leaders who acknowledge and inspire employees when they see the extra effort, get more of that performance in the future. As mentioned, leaders who are efficient at showing gratitude have higher empowerment results, because they are enveloped by a team of experienced professionals who take the initiative and use their abilities to help the company reach a common goal.

It's always beneficial to get some reassurance, encouraged workers are prone to be positive individuals. The latter is dedicated to significant goals and believe that their job is united with their principles and that they can show initiative innovation to accomplish them. Don't concentrate on talent but focus on effort; some companies will even endorse continued education that improves personal development.

When debriefing on a project, be considerate and detailed about the response you provide, these feelings of empowerment will help to clarify the effects of such leaders on both employee imagination and citizenship behavior. Hold an examination meeting after the deadline and be detailed about the measures you'd like to see reiterated and the influence it had on others. As expressed, gratifying positive conduct can be far more efficient than the penalty; to do that, you'll want to offer the team with constructive feedback.

Constructive feedback
When the work atmosphere is constructive, it's easy to overlook insignificant successes in a hectic project where you're continually shifting from one assignment to the next. By communicating some suggestions of positive comments along with the mix, you are confirming that any upcoming projects can be even improved than the one you just completed. Leaders need to bring a constructive approach to work because nobody is perfect, and there will always be room for progress and development. Empowerment must be fostered to develop and thrive; hence, constructive feedback will help employees realize what led to the error and how to prevent making it in the future. Presenting valuable feedback is always beneficial for anyone involved, and the time you dedicate to reward a job well-done is vital for developing an empowered team. For this reason, the desire to establish a great working atmosphere, where people will feel appreciated and let go of meddling to empower your team.

Give team authority and involve them in decision-making
When a team member has the authority to decide, not only can they improve with the success of the project because of their viewpoint,

but they feel more emancipation. Business leaders' value what their employees have to say, and by involving them in such conversations, you're making them realize their significance to the achievement of the project, so asking employees for feedback shows that you value their views. As a leader, you need to acknowledge that employees are valuable resources to business development, not only do you free them to make decisions on the job level but you also pursue discussions about more tactical issues about the project.

By including your team in decision making, you can shine much from their proximity to the development, if you show you are inclined to listen to proposals. It proves that you are passionate about empowering your employees to show off their talent, so they should always be required to present their thoughts about results. You can engage employees in decision making by asking for ideas, the more influential people have over their work and how it is done, the higher their sense of empowerment. The main advantage of having a very emboldened team shows that you are enthusiastic about portioning your leadership role and assigning duties with the group of content people you work with. Leaders are excited to see employees develop; the unrestricted endeavor of employees has a substantial effect on output. Empowerment influences the commitment of the team; therefore, by organizing tasks, you show that you are ready to create new leaders in your business.

Stop Micromanaging

Leaders give employees the independence to come up with inventive concepts on their own; they don't suppress innovation or lower confidence and linger over everything your team members do or make them wretched. A micromanager is a leader who rules everything employees do and does not have adequate self-confidence to distribute responsibilities. If you can't release ideas when reliability has been demonstrated repeatedly, you can discourage employees and result in irritated workers. Employees are competent enough to work autonomously. After they have shown their honesty and expertise, stop micromanaging them. In general, business leaders must be convinced in their hiring decisions, so they know that their employees can get the job done on their own.

Provide Necessary Resources

First, start executing employee empowerment habits by supplying your employees with the knowledge that they need to accomplish on their own. This can also lead to no uncertainty as to the work that you anticipate from your employees and, they will barely visit your offices and anticipate their troubles to be miraculously resolved for them. Resources need to be a sounding panel for suggestions. By doing this, you are providing each member of your staff the chance to thrive at their jobs. As a result, employees trust leaders who they recognized as more inspiring; this will make them feel even more capable and energized when they can achieve it all on their own.

Communicate a Clear Vision

As a leader, being able to connect with employees is an essential leadership value, so it's your job to get everyone on the same page. Leaders are accessible, so let your team know where you want your organization to go, and by clearly conveying the concept of the organization, you are empowering your employees with the information. You can promote a culture of communication by organizing mid-year performance evaluations and identify the responsibilities of your staff. It's becoming more and more crucial for employees to feel like they are supporting to constructing new ideas to the business, so try to have frequent discussions with employees and emphasize that your door is always open. As with anything in life, there will be alterations to your concept, so keep employees informed on what's happening in your business, and employees can feel comfortable discussing with you. As seen, people that do not know what they are expected to be doing won't be able to achieve their jobs very well at all. Still, if they have leaders who are straightforward, positive and truthful, they'll become thrilled about reaching targets and moving for the stars alongside you.

Shared Responsibility
When a leader tries to inspire employees, he or she finds ways to assist each team member in improving and participating through using their powers. Employees will feel encouraged from the start of any project when you ask them to take on extra tasks and charge at work. When you make the decision-making procedure collaborative, your team will feel ownership of that work. Leaders help employees know the company's purpose and concept. Putting the task in the hands of your employees will not only protect you from headaches, but your team members may have more innovative and cost-effective ways to complete a task.

As a leader, empowering control is also about mentoring and encouraging employee growth and recognizing how they are linked to the overall development. You can support employees to find value in their work by adequately coaching them. You need to show employees how their positions fit into reaching your business's objective and working towards your vision. Go over their duties in-depth, then give a list of how it will impact your business development plan; this can encourage them because it reveals that you feel they are valuable and knowledgeable. To explain the effects of empowering leadership on both imagination and social responsibility, designate duties that will allow your team members to flourish and take on additional tasks.

Empowering your team at school

We can map out our management by the techniques in which we inspire others, because leadership is changing from dictating everyone what to do, but instead to encouraging others to come up with the brightest concepts that have never been imagined of before. You make a point of devoting time and means to show your people that you believe in them, in terms of enhancing your sense of self-consciousness and confidence. Empowering other people puts out the optimistic vibes into the environment that will be returned to you. This can be accomplished in several different approaches that can vary from merely lifting someone else's mood to supporting them to recognize new qualities of their personalities. As mentioned, the principle of management is changing from commanding your team can do, to empowering others by discovering how to inspire and encourage them.

Inspiring your team is crucial to developing a high-performance team because they will want to work with you to support you in accomplishing your goals in everything you do. People will do their best for those who care about them, so your capability to procure the expertise, strength, and resources of others allows you to become a proliferation sign. To control yourself so that you achieve far more than the typical person and in a much shorter time, means promoting an atmosphere of confidence and assisting your team learn from achievements and evaluate breakdowns. Empowering underlings isn't easy, though, as a leader, you share your prudence and help others accomplish their goals because it requires that business and their leaders be dedicated to constant team building.

Students Leaders

Provide plenty of opportunities for students to take responsibility. A few questions can get the conversation moving and give you a better understanding of their ideas. How your classroom is structured can hinder student leadership. Thus, gain better knowledge about your students, whether that's through group activities or clarifying an idea they've understood to the rest of the class. Students should want to find their voice, at the opening of each semester, to allow students to express their views about how they would like to learn and make it constructive knowledge. One of the easiest ways to inspire students is by promoting leadership performances, therefore, give students a chance to make their own decision.

Students decision-making power
One of the most significant ways to empower students is to offer them alternatives for how they might submit their tasks and evaluations to you and the class. This might seem like an abstract concept in the age of ordinary basic guidelines. Students will pick the technique that will help them learn the material better, and this student-directed syllabus theory is appropriate to many other subjects. Giving students the authority to decide generates a sense of ownership over the learning and drives them outside of their comfort zone. Therefore, students should be given the liberty not only to express what they believe but also to articulate it however they prefer.

Involve students in real-world issues
It can create a barrier for student emancipation if what they learn isn't relevant to life outside the classroom. Teachers must connect the outside humankind to the school, therefore, have students exercise abilities they've come to understand in-service education or by having views on "real" topics like education transformation. The students are civil to each other, and parents are okay, policymaking can be one of the most stimulating subjects there is for students if you stay neutral. For this reason, have your students make a change with what they've discovered, when students know their learning has significance

beyond exams and classes, they'll be more encouraged to study further.

Help students succeed
Enthusiastic people don't remain silent for long, so give students a way to link what they're passionate about with their experiments. Bringing the age group of your learners into account by establishing a platform for them to convey a positive opinion, helps you improve your teaching. Partnering with students in leading the learning process shows them the vital role they play in their education, stressing that education is about collaboration. Incorporating student empowerment activities in the classroom are important, so find a cause that benefits them and concentrate on it in your curricula as the main topic for a few days. Overall, find out what your students are passionate about; these principles can enhance learning results at the school and district level as well.

Share exceptional work
For more significant projects and assignments, share successful assignments with the rest of the class. Sometimes, students can learn more from each other than when they just listen to their teacher, so let students know that you will choose a few standouts to be shared with the class. This encourages students to put more into their work when they see that they may get to share it with their peers; it stirs self-confidence when their assignments are chosen to be the best. By selecting individual students to share their work, it gives them a chance to demonstrate their knowledge. Alternatively, you can set up discussion groups of students to share what they've learned in front of the class, students discussing their work with their peers is an ideal way for them to grasp concepts. As expressed, this idea of recounting what they've learned will mark effects. You will concurrently

stimulate self-assurance in those students and encourage other students to do their best in their schoolwork.

Use meaningful technology
Technology is becoming more and more essential in schools as it develops and progresses; it can be very empowering to use it in class. Possibly one of the best instruments accessible for supporting student voice, by having your students bring their gadgets, you open a circle of new learning prospects, and you confirm that learning can occur anytime, anywhere. Technology allows students to communicate and submit their work to the whole classroom; it sets education power in our hands, and to encourage and share and files is a relatively well-established practice in the classroom. This makes both great forums for teaching and student partnership when students use their gadgets during class time to retrieve learning resources that they can also get at home. Therefore, technology is likely the most effective way a student can link up with other people. It helps them make their work more appealing and collaborative.

Personal Empowerment
No one is born feeling self-empowered if we want to make a change in the world to possibility, collaboration, and achievement, we need to work to make a substantial change. Self-confidence is discovered by giving yourself the juice you need to achieve your objectives and live your desires. You can inspire yourself by concentrating on what you can control and your devotion to keeping a purpose and energized attitude. You can begin today to crawl your way to developing self-empowered, and love what you do so profoundly that you can involve others in your vision and empower them in their achievement. Our mindset can suddenly change from pessimistic to optimistic with persistence and endurance. As a result, to live an empowered life of significant impact, we need to build both the core

and external conditions that will sustain us in making the most significant influence.

> *"We must look for ways to be an active force in our own lives. We must take charge of our own destinies, design a life of substance and truly begin to live our dreams"* (Les Brown, 2020).

Individuals who are empowered don't fall apart under failure, but they have an inspiring influence on all those who surround them. During stressful moments, love what you do so sincerely that there will be no adversity that will take you from your chosen path and focus on what you earn from experience rather than on what you lose. Nobody feels excellent, but some of us amplify our shortcomings more than others, so you can connect with daily reminders that you are resilient and competent in many ways. Below are a few short recommendations you can encourage yourself to generate a significant difference and start to sparkle more brilliantly.

Run Your Race
Don't value other people's views before you listen to yourself. It's ok to take a moment to feel sorrow or whatever sentiments you may be going through. Allow yourself to understand your preliminary reaction. It's your life, so focus on your race. Most people listen to others, instead of fretting about the competition, concentrate on the ball that is right in front of you. Another person's achievement does not compare as your failure when you talk down your powers to others. You may end up suppressing this idea and miscalculating your ability. You will miss your way of the significance of what you're doing, if you are concerned about the competition, so inspire yourself in the same way that you would a close friend. Empowerment has

nothing to do with race, dedicate yourself to a routine that helps maintain you in touch with this grounded state of life, and come up with ways you make the world a better place.

Trust Yourself
Trust enables you to move determinedly in the direction of your objectives, so you need to know where your accountability ends, and someone else's begins, then immerse yourself in learning everything you need to know about your interests. You are liable for your contentment, but if you waste your time questioning your abilities, then you can't contribute to happiness because the only point you will be actively achieving is your capability to question yourself. You must prove to yourself that you have what it takes to be creative when going for your ambitions, and experience will give you the power you need to support you be the best you can be. Change all that time, concentrating on questioning yourself to believing in yourself. You can start by trying one concept and put it in action. Recognizing our weaknesses can help us come closer to meeting our full capacity, you will realize to trust yourself the most profoundly through taking determined action-driven possibilities. Therefore, believe that you have what it takes to get the job done, and how to switch from each position.

Love What You Do
Love is the most influential of all the sentiments, try to think about what kinds of things make you happy, and do something communicative every day. Trust that you will be the best at what motivates your heart the most, which is why truly energized people work in professions they love. No one can do it all. Be aware the next time you're doing something and get a fire burning in your heart, then you must do it regularly. It must be something you enjoy, so it is best

to concentrate on one or two things you can do well, and then devote entirely to your source.

Unforeseen situations might blow you back a bit along your route, but you need to think about how you can best make a change. Maybe you can give your time to help the situation directly, but it will not have the power to take you from your goal. Most will do almost anything for love, take note the next time you find yourself working on something for hours and work doesn't feel like work, but more personal. When you are genuinely passionate about what you want, the more excited you will be about continuing to create change. Focus on issues that speak to your heart and fears you may have of failing will be outdone by the passion you have never to let failing to be an option; that's your strength. Overall, the more you feel and see yourself making a difference, that is the gift God has given you. Make sure to pursue it to feel empowered

Embrace Imperfect Moments

The most vested way to victory comes through your encounters of disappointment, which are measures or diversions, but valid actions on your path. While it is important to feel these events fully, when faced with a challenging situation, try to focus on what you can affect. Every obstacle is an opportunity to discover your abilities and flourish from that experience. Still, you will lose your control when you let feelings of fear supplant our capability to act. Liberation is most intensely developed during times of difficulties, and you can't succeed without taking chances, so when faced with a significant change, take time to look at the positive outcomes from challenging situations. Even in failure or tragedy, you can't take risks without occasionally failing, so think about the last time you thrived under new circumstances and how you built your coping skills and life perspective.

> *"It is God who arms me with strength and makes my way perfect"* (Psalms 18:32 NKJV HolyBible, 2020).

Disappointment and doubt are the new mindsets that will empower you to strive for positive change in your life, and it is an essential structure for you to bounce against the wall for the enhancement of your refinement. Your imperfect moments give the ideal path for your progress, but you'll never get there if you let the fear of failing prevent you from starting to walk. As seen, without failure, you would have nothing to improve upon, the essential things in our lives often come from the most intense growing pains, therefore, choose to grow rather than disappear under stress.

Network
One of the quickest approaches to move your objective ahead is to find people devoted to your cause and develop on the power that comes from working together for a higher purpose. Sometimes we are afraid to act alone, so to empower yourself, you need to collaborate and don't compete. Success is never a one-person job. Remember that we can do more together through networking. Enthusiasm exceeds disappointment, so mobilize a team of people who have a strong point to fill in where you have weaknesses, since we are empowered by this connection and collaboration with others. The achievement will always attract haters, but there is nothing that can get in your way when you want something badly enough. Continue to harness the power of the community. I'm a big believer in using my strengths and the gifts God has given me; thus, in collaborative environments, success is shared. Collaboration is about inclusion that helps with feelings of isolation and helplessness. It is people empowering other people. For this reason, broadening your sense of community allows you to delegate out to those who can best help you reach your goals.

NOTES

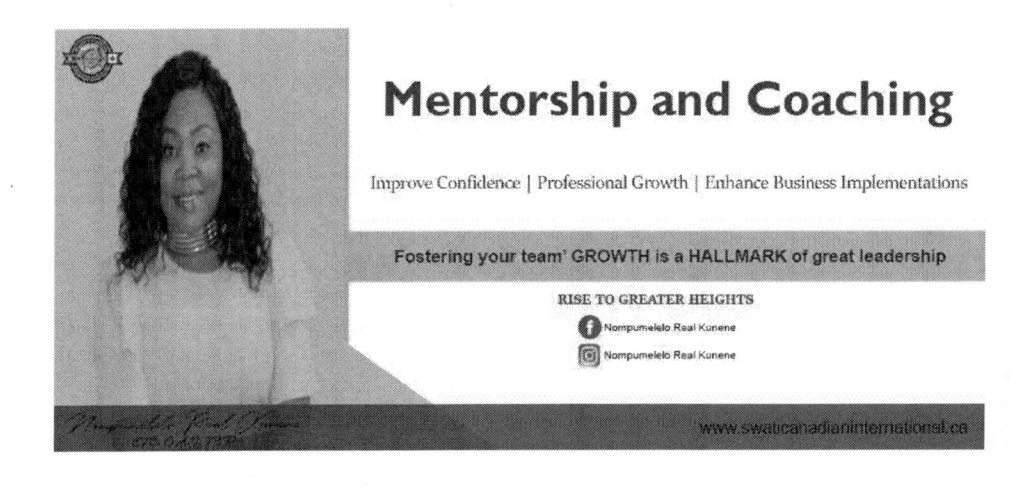

Mentorship and Coaching

Improve Confidence | Professional Growth | Enhance Business Implementations

Fostering your team' GROWTH is a HALLMARK of great leadership

RISE TO GREATER HEIGHTS

Nompumelelo Real Kunene
Nompumelelo Real Kunene

www.swaticanadianinternational.ca

Chapter 11

MENTORSHIP AND COACHING

Businesses can be entirely changed with the proper coaching and mentoring approaches, hence the application of coaching and mentoring in the business becomes an exceptional impact to the overall growth of the individual and organisations. The advantages of mentoring and coaching are diverse and can certainly influence an individual's profession if they are connecting with their coach, it also provides employees a path to connect and flourish within the company and along their own career paths. For this reason, if you have knowledge in a position that someone else would like to learn more about, mentoring and coaching will be worth the time investment, as it empowers both individual and corporate clients to accomplish their full ability.

"Give instruction to a wise man, and he will be still wiser; Teach a just man, and he will increase in learning"
(Proverbs 9:9 NKJV, HolyBible, 2020).

Coaching and mentoring are practices that create methods to involve your staff in regulating stretch-goals and delivers an atmosphere where professionals of every sector generate concepts to develop each other up. Both coaching and mentoring can enhance an immense amount of value to organisations, therefore these plans are integrated as a normal procedure in the organisational structure in the present time. Coaching and mentoring your employees need a constant attempt to make it a part of your leadership procedures, such as employees who need to improve their abilities, working performance failures and difficulties with routine production.

Coaching or mentoring produces substantial benefits to the organization, and it is accomplished when the executive notices that there are employees who must enhance their abilities to achieve better in their jobs by being more productive. Everybody likes feeling like an essential part of a team, thus mentoring or coaching can help to develop a constructive and tangible change in individual and build efficient communication abilities. Coaching has been known to improve confidence to enhance work implementation, and mentoring is a great way to get an employee more engaged at work. In case of organisations and companies, coaching and mentoring become deeply valuable to enhance the transfer of expertise from the coach/mentor to the employee.

Advice for Mentees

While mentorship can be an incredible career fuel, being mentored is one of the most valuable development prospects you can get, but for the company to get the appropriate advisor can be a hard. Honesty is key for the connection to flourish, having the leadership and encouragement of a skilled mentor can provide a mentee with a comprehensive range of professional benefits. Mentees are more likely to buy into the mentor's concept and go the extra mile to win, this is crucial, because mentees must keep in mind that mentors are doing this from the kindness of their heart. As a result, being a good mentee is the best way to make sure the rapport enjoys a healthy resolute existence, since these all open gates to better liaisons with management and a more competent labor force.

- Coaching and mentoring offer useful guidance on improving strengths and surmounting difficulties outside of direct line management, so mentees must be dedicated to developing their abilities and focus on attaining professional outcomes.
- Mentees need to be sure about their career aspirations to gain support on professional growth and innovation. They must be

clear about what they want to get from mentoring to become more emboldened to make decisions.
- Mentors can help with problem solving particularly across professional growth, so mentees must be receptive to trying new concepts. This is the opportunity to create approaches for dealing with personal concerns by discovering various avenues perceptions.
- Experience to new concepts of thinking can increase your self-confidence because mentors want to see progress and development. Be personally accountable to obtain important insight into the next phase of your profession.
- Be dedicated to maintaining your end of the deal to cultivate a longer-term supportive rapport.
- Recognize goals and create a sense of control which will boost recognition within the company.

Advice for Mentors
Mentoring is more than the transfer of information, expertise and perceptions, it involves a commitment to replicate on and share one's own skills, including one's disappointments. Mentors may be hesitant to devote to a mentorship plan due to time limitations, but the relationship presents mutual benefits for mentors eager to invest their time in building another professional. Good mentors must be able to walk the talk with their personal fulfilment of sharing their knowledge to cultivate other people. Being engaged in mentoring offers some substantial benefits that can reward mentors professionally and seeing company development improves with the repercussions of a profitable mentoring programme. In general, abilities and knowledge differ significantly between various generations and the position of a mentor is to inspire the personal and professional advancement of a mentee through the sharing of experience.

Mentors may be concerned whether they really have something valuable to share, but the reality is that mentoring offers personal satisfaction through encouraging the growth of others, and benefit from a sense of satisfaction and personal development. They should be confident that their knowledge is appreciated because they will create approaches for dealing with both personal and academic matters which will expose them to fresh viewpoints, concepts and methods. The best teachers have always been those who remain interested novices themselves, so mentoring will empower you as a mentor to exercise and improve your social abilities which will give you a chance to reflect on your own objectives and improve your inspiration.

If they have been with the organization for a long time, mentors can be distinguished for their subject knowledgeable and it uses your accumulated knowledge, making it accessible to a new person, then you will become more energized to make judgments.

Mentoring takes time, it's more important to have someone who can give guidance in areas where you experience some difficulties. A commitment to share disappointments and personal encounters can provide significant support for mentees at critical moments in their life, it offers the mentor a chance to reflect on own mentoring tactics and gain acknowledgment for their competences. The capability and readiness to dedicate strength to the mentoring relationship provides useful prospects for a growth mindset and knowledge approach. Their mentee could inspire you to think more profoundly about a new focus, which will strengthen your study abilities and understanding of their subject to enhance communication abilities.

Benefits for The Company

Coaching and mentoring staff makes them more critical to your organization, thus investing in it is a beneficial way to build your top evolving ability by improving their skills. By being involved in the development of your staff, you're showing them that you care about their improvement, and employees who undertake training become more accountable in finding their results, having less dependency on their line manager. Observing your employees as they develop over a long period can help you make vital business choices that will enhance staff confidence and implementation, contributing to the more significant usage of abilities. We all have hidden talents; coaching helps people determine their enthusiasm as it plugs into their fundamental ideals that they can bring in more revenue and make it simpler for your business to pay for coaching expenses.

Significance Coaching and Mentoring

Coaching and mentoring are merely understanding that someone is there explicitly to help a mentee to ask questions about the abilities they need to flourish in that exact instant. Goal attainment is an essential part of the improvement to the atmosphere and having assistance for enhancing skills can be very useful. Mentoring is a more intimate form of training that encompasses pairing knowledge of skilled professionals with people that could use help adapting to their chosen profession. It can help benefit the mentor as well, because coaching is a talent, too, and one that develops with practice.

As competence building is often the core of mentoring relationships, when we teach, we often teach others what we most want to understand ourselves, so there should be a specific significance on which skills to cultivate so the teaching is efficient and pursued. Overall, driven encouragement will make the mentoring relationship effective in its goals, we become more mindful of our own considerations, not just how to convey what we understand to new and diverse audiences.

Mentoring often comes in part when a new employee can gain from personal support on duties. This can help lessen disappointments on a personal level and enhance the work satisfaction of the individual, presenting a benefit for the company. A leader's first-hand experience is also precious, so small businesses can also use coaches to help build other workers along a career path. Such as management, because there are circumstances to the company that an employee will face that they won't get in any book, and this will lead to better productivity across the company. Coaching lets individuals to settle matters within the limits of intimate connection; this can consist of pairing a mentor or coach with new employees to settle into the surroundings. On top of enhancing employees, coaching and mentoring involves participants with its distinctive one-on-one feedback, which allows leaders to recognize the limitations and strengths of each employee. As expressed, it's vital to give positive feedback and ideas for ways to improve themselves to a mentee.

Coaching and mentoring can provide a multitude of advantages. It gives the individual a secure space to go and discuss delicate matters. On an organizational level, having a coach isn't just about enhancing an individual's abilities in the workplace; it takes knowledge to an even higher intensity. Through coaching, an individual can discover more about themselves. They may feel a better sense of dedication to the business. When knowledgeable professionals provide opportunities for mentees, they may find out how they are understood by others and develop on areas of their characters that they are not satisfied with.

Further, coaching takes knowledge to a degree beyond learning; once the individual is at ease with their abilities, they can start to utilize them in their professions. As seen, training helps an employee feel comfortable with leadership, and it can help promote loyalty to the company, resulting in invaluable work experience.

Launching a Mentoring Program

Mentoring is a recognized tactic to run robust development for both mentees and mentors, so the initial measure about launching a mentoring program is to outline the purpose of the plan. If you are aiming to cultivate leaders, starting this program might be the closest you'll ever get to making a business determination that has solely constructive influence. Unlike comparable learning motivations like offering to pay for programs, mentoring improves retention and employee fulfilment. Mentoring can enhance employee contentment by using the resources that your company already has and makes your business more enticing to individuals who might be interested in joining.

Mentoring or coaching is a substantial venture when you consider program management and the valuable time of participants. The leaders of the organization should take part in a significant role in this, conveying the influence is vital to ensure continuing support. Knowing how your program measures up to anticipations may well be the most crucial phase of all. You need to explain to individuals why they should decide to join and help them see the idea of why it matters. To be efficient, you need the capability to secure metrics and feedback throughout the program development. You also need to make sure that senior executives within the organization are on-board and are part of the communications that go out. Overall, there is usually natural excitement if the mentoring program is pursued, assessed, and measured.

When new mentoring programs are presented in organizations, and once you are determined what objectives a mentoring program can accomplish for your company, set up a plan that suits your company culture. Leaders in your company must make it clear that they think the program is essential. If you want constructive outcomes, arrange a mentoring workflow for participants to play a part in the program, it is also important to help participants attain valuable learning that achieves specified goals. Don't assume prospective participants in your company know the benefits, find people in your company. They are eager to share the mentoring practices that have made a constructive impression on their jobs.

"Every decision you need to make, every task you need to accomplish, every relationship you need to navigate, every element of daily life you need to traverse, God has already perfectly matched up with an equivalent-to-overflowing supply of His grace. If you don't agree with that, then you either lack a proper appreciation for what you have, or you are doing things that you're not supposed to be participating in right now"
(Priscilla Shirer, 2011).

The most excellent planned coaching programs will not go far without efficient mentor recruitment, then you can start your plan slowly. At the program intensity, build metrics around defined business objectives. Still, it's beneficial to at least make a recommendation for how the mentoring team-up can get the most out of their rapport. Mentoring or coaching pairs might choose to plan their time otherwise depending on their objectives and preferences, so beyond participants, main leaders will need to be informed on the advantages of the program and tactical significance to the organization.

For mentoring relationships, you want to know mentorship performance to pinpoint barriers and opportunities because participants will bring a variety of skills, experiences, and desires. Look at efficiency and quantifiable progress in the areas that your program is pursuing and assess several match combinations before confirming because ensuring quality mentors and hard-to-match mentees can be difficult.

Even if a company puts you together with your mentor, create clear boundaries with your mentees and do not assume that you are both on the same page for a productive relationship. Let your mentor know your schedule and what you are expecting to get out of the mentorship. Boundaries can form a professional and long-lasting relationship. Occasionally your mentor may think you want guidance on stepping up in the organization, so explain your outlooks.

In conclusion
Mentoring/Coaching is an impactful approach to build, connect, and maintain your people, but developing a strong foundation of mentors can be a challenge. When running an efficient mentoring program, it is vital to know the constructive and undesirable aspects that influence mentor involvement. Have a proper procedure that creates closure to the mentoring knowledge. A great notion is to establish a program workflow map to clarify each phase of your program. Offer an opportunity for both the mentor and mentee to reflect upon what was learned, then give details such as critical measures, backing resources, and standards for going to the next level.

When an individual becomes connected with their workplace, it allows the organization to exploit the resources at hand to keep the whole team working efficiently, which can enhance the role of the entire organization. The level of commitment individuals achieve in their coaching connections can help to improve retention levels and efficiency, advancing their careers as well as their overall organization. For a real impact on your organization, look for innovative ways to strengthen positive drivers, and reduce the obstacles through determination and resources.

NOTES

STRATEGIES FOR GROWING YOUR CHURCH

Challenge People to Serve

Create a Welcoming Experience
Invest in Children's and Youths Ministry
Accessibility on Social Media
Cell Groups

RISE TO GREATER HEIGHTS

- Nompumelelo Real Kunene (Facebook)
- Nompumelelo Real Kunene (Instagram)

www.swaticanadianinternational.ca

Chapter 12

STRATEGIES FOR GROWING YOUR CHURCH

One purpose that many churches concentrate on is growth, and they play an extremely vital position in millions of people's souls. Churches want to reach out to more people, and influencing more saints is an outcome of development. Thus, you need to examine your position as pastor the moment you choose that you want to grow your church. Building a church entails an idea and strategy to offer people the ability to connect with Christ, which means that you must be willing to change from minister to leader to lead successfully. As the pastor of a small congregation, even if you know everyone and guide everybody personally, you need to outline the stages to grow and implement your tactical idea.

> "Therefore, take heed to yourselves and to all the flock, among which the Holy Spirit has made you overseers, to shepherd the church of God which He purchased with His own blood" (Acts 20:28 NKJV HolyBible, 2020).

The earliest Christians had no knowledge of what a church development approach was, yet many churches today must formulate and transcribe church objectives for the year to come. Still, there's a boundary to how many people they can personally guide. If everything depends on you, you become an impediment to growth because you must personally minister to every person in your church. You must be prepared to allow other people to contribute to the ministry because the church cannot flourish beyond your own strength intensity. If you're questioning what you need to do to grow,

I've put together some approaches to help you increase your church attendance, strengthen your ministry, and connect with new audiences for your church. Let's discover these tactics to drive commitment at your church that can support you break an attendance hurdle.

Make the Decision to Grow
Having a well-outlined concept, purpose, and principles statement establish the path for any organization. Believe it or not, the main obstacle to church growth is an aspiration. The critical aim people frequently go to church is to feel closer to God, but it's no secret that that number of people who go to church isn't on the rise. For a church to grow, you need to build a spirit that's more like a church plant. No matter how recognized your church is, if you want to see fast consequences, some things must die, for example, those who had intimacy with the pastor must learn to share him with new people. If you're a pastor or a church leader, you may have observed a decline in your community, and you perhaps find yourself wondering where you're missing the mark. Churches are enthused enough to send their pastor to church development meetings. Still, if only the pastor and a few families are devoted to the development, then you will experience some effort. It's going to be a demanding climb. For this reason, it takes unbelievable selflessness. You need to have the motivation for constant enactment to church growth.

Challenge People to Serve
At the heart of all of us is a need to serve others, so persuading people to volunteer may be more valuable than urging them to join a group. Be prepared to give up some leadership and assign ministry to the people in the seats; people who assist in the operation are involved in the mission. We need to be offered with prospects to help other people, and you can do this by connecting volunteer and ministry opportunities more rapidly. After the congregation has determined it

wants to grow, then help your people realize that they'll have to do their part in ministry by sharing their distinctive talents and organize them to start ministering. For this to work, opportunities to serve offers members the ability to use their gifts to help God's people, so everyone needs to be prepared to pull out information casually. In general, whether it is serving meals to the less privileged or assisting others in a time of the disaster, your purpose is to get everyone into a group, and they should also have a working understanding of church members and their inclinations.

"There is nothing I'm any more passionate than empowering the next generation" (Bishop T.D. Jakes, 2020).

Create A Welcoming Experience

Everybody wants to be welcomed, but not everyone is comfortable being deluged with unwanted attention, so do all you can to make new guests feel at home. People are naturally attracted to a visually attractive atmosphere, placing personal invitation cards on every chair in the hall for people to use, will boost the possibility that they'll return next Sunday if you also highlight on the cards at every service. It is unfortunate, but true that we are a customer-focused culture, so remember to follow up with first-time visitors and make it a collaborative endeavor to greet your new members as soon as they walk through your doors. Remember, improving your church and the whole community is a fantastic way to enhance relationships with new members. It is also one of the essential keys to growing church attendance. Therefore, focus on your Sunday morning welcome because it can have a significant effect on your congregation; it is also ideal for churches looking to attract and keep guests.

Provide A Clear Path Toward Involvement

The splendor of the body of Christ is that God utilizes everyone in a somewhat unique way, but the difficulty for many people who join in a church is that they don't know what to do to be engaged. Having a mission statement is essential, and those distinctive traits that your congregation holds will let the community congregate around a mutual goal and concept. Most flourishing churches promote a straightforward tactical method that pushes people through the phases of spiritual growth, which is what God utilizes to build a beautiful tapestry of churches. Your mission statement must make expansion the primary concern, the clearer the way is toward in commitment, the more people will travel it. Construct around a growth-focused concept, and naturally accelerate the church's aim and dream. If the leadership and the church are clear about the development, it will be accessible using the people God has planted in the local congregation to be used by God with their distinctive talents.

We are all on a journey, and the group supports us grow our exceptional calling as Christians. Thus, church development is not about competing with the church down the street. Overall, I believe people are called to churches for an objective, so try to assist people in connecting.

Invest in children and youth ministries

Church's position in the lives of children is one of its significant draws to expand involvement and develop an involved community successfully. Hence, you need to generate training that relates directly to your youth and children. Assigning the youth and children with responsibilities will also show them the power of worship and, you'll be so amazed that people who've lost contact with the church in their teens have kids, discover themselves wanting the congregation to influence their children. Some millennials say they don't go to church because it's not directly applicable to them, so make sure to let them stay convinced in your capability to love and minister to in their lives. If you want to appeal to young families who are re-imagining church, you don't want to seem disorganized because when children and teens are thrilled about your ministry, they'll share the information with their friends. When it comes to finding this area squared away, and investment in young people is an asset in the potential of your church community.

Increase Your Accessibility on Social Media

Notwithstanding their best goals, even the most reliable congregants can't make it to church every Sunday, so give prospective participants a sneak preview of what they can anticipate by sharing inspiring videos from your sermons on social media. With your words, you can make it clear that the purpose of the Christian belief is to do something with what you know; this will help circulate your objective and the word about your church. Not that you need to nail people every week, but you can make use of social media to provide people knowledge, or you can use it to call people to act. One of the biggest desires of the human soul is to feel genuinely fit in, so presenting your congregants the opportunity to stream your sermons live is a great way to link them to their faith culture.

Intimacy grows in small groups

The congregation speaks a lot about the transformative power of people; you must plan for the development and plan out what your requirements will be. People ultimately comply with the standards beliefs, so an excellent small group entails participation from everyone, which generates a sense of ownership. Jesus holds up Christian devotion as the evidence that we are his followers. However, it's hard enough for the members of your church to bring in more followers, so when it comes to building an energized community that draws newcomers, congregation cell groups are crucial.

Make it as simple as possible for individuals to share their belief when you don't expect people to do more than to join your congregation, don't be amazed if all they do is go to your church and not getting involved. Compassionate is a genuine issue; people become devoted to their church's purpose and vision. Thus small groups become the instruments for looking after the body. Consider having multiplication of cell groups. Saints will experience the transforming strength of the community. They become devoted to the church in remarkable ways. It's essential to bear in mind that you should never assume someone will be present. If you want your church to have a more significant influence and experience more remarkable growth, try delivering more sermons, and making them more concise.

Conclusion
Devoting time with God is what drives the call and the anointing to do what needs to be done in a congregation, so I believe that, with a revived devotion to the original message of Jesus Christ by your church, the best days of the community are beyond it. If God called you into ministry, don't take that call lightly, I believe that there are still millions of lives prepared to join the considerable shadow of witnesses, so devote time with him, and he will show you in the path you should take. We are on Jesus's side, and we have a crucial role to play in sorting that party out, therefore, write the idea down and diagram out a strategy to carry out God's work– theological church growth is inevitable!

NOTES

WAYS TO TRUST GOD WITH YOUR TROUBLES

Have Faith
Wait Patiently
Pray
Remain Hopeful

Bonus 1

WAYS TO TRUST GOD WITH YOUR TROUBLES

"I waited patiently for the LORD; And He inclined to me, and heard my cry. He also brought me up out of a horrible pit, out of the miry clay, and set my feet upon a rock, and established my steps" (Psalms 40:1-2 NKJV HolyBible, 2020).

David starts this psalm proclaiming that he is anticipating patiently for the Lord, followed by a joint statement of Jehovah's righteousness to his saints. Even though he was being punished by the Lord, exasperation never lingered in his heart, much less fled his mouth, but David is tolerantly waiting for these things to end. It is an excellent illustration of the manner that God carries out his policies and objectives in each of our lives, and there is enough power in God to support those who are not strong enough to stand. We go to a fast-food restaurant, and we anticipate the food to be served promptly and effectively, but God does things in his way and his ideal moment. Many others happen to trust God when they realize this pattern of life, the gloom of essence under the spirit of God's withdrawals, is indeed a terrible pit and miry clay. Worries and anxieties about the immortal state, are a horrible pit and miry clay, but God does this to cultivate our trust in his word.

Patient waiting upon God was a unique trait of our Lord Jesus, although it might not be a vicious wresting of language to see both David and his Lord. Psalm 40 is a song of admiration for our God. The notion of David waiting on or for the Lord has been ordinary. Trusting God is a challenging factor for many people, and David has proffered advice to those in the same situations as David to wait for the Lord (39:2). This understanding of prayer is what we must all go through, though we live in a culture that says that we must see outcomes, and we need to see them immediately. It should seem David wrote this psalm upon a circumstance of his liberation, of what the Lord has offered for him directly, by the superpower and kindness of God. Jesus is here, we all must convey our problems to God, and hence we shall let the sunshine even though this should suppress the stars. David may have penned it during his hard refugee years or maybe during the early years of his supremacy because he waited intently on the Lord to save him from the first pit. As expressed, this beautiful Psalm of David is a triumphant declaration to Israel, from some impressive and pressing difficulty, by which he was in risk of being swamped.

The psalmist remained hopeful and praying. I see that the Lord, suppose he glides and slow down the impact of his servant's supplication, and grants not his wish at first, yet he hears him. There is a humankind of disparity between swamp and pillar, but those that wait patiently for God do not wait in futile. When he comes, he will lighten us out of the ditch. By the mercy of God, people have been comforted by a sense of hopelessness with a sense of reassurance. Christ is the pillar on which a weak heart can only stand firm, and he carries the royal trophy among the persistent. His anguish on the cross was a terrible pit and miry clay, but no glimpse of fury and no act of revenge came from God's long-suffering lamb. This is relevant to Christ. He waited and was unflappable to precision, far surpassing all others who have, according to their gauge, praised God in the difficult situations.

Unsurprisingly, our displeasure carries us to hopelessness and predominant worries about the immortal life. Still, God can change us when he comes, and he will establish our feet upon a pillar where no situations can stir us. The great pain that the psalmist had been in, he defines his agony as getting blows from a hand, and in which he found himself sinking yet further. Where God has given steadfast hope, suppose he delay the effect of your prayers, he expects there should be a steady, regular walk and conduct. God filled the psalmist with joy, as well as peace in believing and thinking that he defers the impact and power thereof, nevertheless pray without ceasing. We have learned to fear justice, but God makes us realize that he has heard our prayers, and to enlarge our trust in His never-failing goodness and grace. When you wait patiently for the Lord, you might be convinced that this potency is provided of God, and by faith beholding the sufferings and glory of Christ.

All of us have and will endure times that are indeed the pits, just as David describes. But many are the benefits with which we are daily loaded, both by the providence and by the grace of God. In the pit, we had not forgotten God, but if the heart understands that the Lord has rejected our prayer altogether, it is not possible to continue in prayer. Life tosses us curveballs, and we don't get what we always want in life, but when we know that the Lord hears us, suppose he delays, let us crave perseverance to accept his goodwill.

Many times, we must deal with the pits of immorality, and one of the ways God holds us up is by allowing us to hit the pits, abandoning us there a while, and then getting us out into his kindness again. The psalmist realized that he could have faith in God by waiting patiently for him to answer his prayers. We can find ourselves trapped in the muddiness of immorality. Many times, one sin leads to another sin, and we have great trouble trying to extricate ourselves from the mud. The support we need is not merely one another, because we are in our slippery pits of transgression. Each of us must call to the Lord to help us out of our chaos. All of us descend to that situation because of our fallen spirit. Maybe what we are to think is sinking into a well and falling deep in the mud at the base but believing God with our prayers means that we also have confidence in him with our praise.

Whatever the condition was, David is recounting how he prayed, waited, and trusted God with his prayers. You may have asked yourself that why you should have faith in God if you are going to go through all of the sorts of obstacles in life and going deeper every time you attempt to raise a foot, and then unexpectedly, there is thunderous water coming from somewhere. It flashes around you in the darkness. It makes it easier to see ourselves in the trenches with the king, but one of the more challenging pits to extricate ourselves from our damaging practices. We have behaviors that are very hard to handle and difficult to break. Still, anything that triggers a sense of vulnerability and hopelessness jeopardizes to destroy life—that is, the king's pit. We all must deal with practices that are not appropriate to break them, but only the word of Christ puts a song in a person's heart. Many instances, our fight is dealing with disappointment, but God can bring us from every sort of pit if we have prepared our hearts to yearn to be like God. When you have Christ in your heart, something transforms inside of you. Thus, we must submit our disappointments in life to the Lord.

The Lord Jehovah made David climb from all his humiliation. Perhaps it was some difficulty of mind arising from a sense of immorality and of God's anger against him for it. When our Lord suffered in his person the horrible affliction which was due to sin, the Son of David was brought exceptionally low, but he rose to triumph. He was so cast down as to be like an inmate in a frightening prison, but the Saviour's prayers among the midnight in Gethsemane teaches us how to conduct our disputes to thrive after the same splendid form of victory. David accounts God's favor to him in bringing him out of his deep anguish. He repeated his steps from that deep hell of sorrow into which he had been hurled as our substitute with gratitude to his praise.

"Even when you cannot see the future, you can know that God is already there" (Debbie Lindell, 2019).

On many occasions, the situations of our lives are the pits, but there are at least two critical aspects in the manner we should wait with the king: humbleness and optimism. Psalm 37:9 and 2 Corinthians 4:8-9 shows that those who remain are the meek, after finding themselves in dreadful situations. For this reason, waiting for the Lord is a significant part of the Christian life, and we shall never wait upon the Lord in vain.

I want to adhere to David's strategy for stepping out of a pit and what we are meant to feel with the king when we understand that it is like being stuck in a desolate miry clay. This psalm suggests not only an upbeat agony but as though David cried out of the deepest despair in the lack of reliable comfort by which sadness might have been declared acceptable. What a marvel is it that our redeemer who, for our sake, was robbed of all solace while encircled with every form of despair. When you're in the pit, wait strictly on the Lord, and you will receive the father's support after the same method of belief.

God has pledged in his promises to be an ever-present help in times of difficulty, so it is a beautiful thing when a broken man sincerely cries out to the Lord. Jesus is the true Joseph taken from the pit to be Lord of all, and we have his promised confidence that his help will come at the perfect time. He does not offer his support immediately, but if we surrender our troubles to the Lord, we shall by faith soar to hold on the same exalted pillar of heavenly favor. What a reassurance to know that Jesus' generous plan of salvation and his faithfulness are not likely to be cut short by disappointment in years to come, for God has fixed him steadfastly.

Each time we encounter God's liberation, we stand in astonishment, because beautiful things can occur in our lives when we put our faith in the Lord. God's deliverance is plentiful, as David turns his cries to the Lord, the Lord responds by turning to David, seeing his predicament and hearing his call. We need God's deliverance in many ways at different seasons. God will turn to us and hear our cry when we get closer to him. God can perform miracles in our lives. He will deliver you in some situations that may look impossible in our eyes. God's freedom is available. He can be a substitute to help us conquer our vicious behaviors. We incline to think God cannot make these drastic shifts in our lives, but eventually, the disciple of the Lord Jesus Christ will encounter God's deliverance from sin in God's perfect timing.

NOTES

Can Single Parents be successful?
Yes...
You can be a SINGLE PARENT
&
make MILLIONS
whilst raising your LITTLE ONES!
Wear the HUSTLER Role
Look for MOTIVATION
Be CHEERFUL
Ban Toxic PEOPLE
RISE TO GREATER HEIGHTS
Nompumelelo Real Kunene
Nompumelelo Real Kunene
Nompumelelo Real Kunene
CTC, SAM, TCP
www.swaticanadianinternational.ca

Bonus 2

CAN SINGLE PARENTS BE SUCCESSFUL?

Many single parents often find themselves deluged by economic pressures, and their added obligation presents an even steeper task. Very seldom do you get encouraging views of single parents as self-sufficient, productive contributors to society. That reputation comes with an inbuilt power for business achievement. Sometimes life happens, and we don't get a say on the roads we take, but the Lord welcomes the single parent with his amazing and generous love. As a single-mom entrepreneur, operating a business is a ton of work, but it doesn't mean that you should be demoted in the community and looked down on.

The humankind is failing to recognize a single parent the way she is, but instead, they will be labelling her. Let's clear some things up about single parents: many things are difficult about raising kids alone. However, they're not dreadfully lonely. Being a single mother is not an easy job, but you discover profound powers and abilities you never knew you had. Life is all about finding new things daily, and being a single parent is twice the work, which makes you stronger. The primary battle of single parents is juggling a lot and working long hours striving to find the time and the strength to do all that they need to do. Don't get me wrong. I know raising a child on your own can be challenging; however, don't let the opinion of this lifestyle count you out before you even count yourself in. Overall, being a single parent comes with a variety of competencies that do well in entrepreneurship, and achievement means being the best parent your kids can have and living your dreams while at it.

Being a single parent is not something that any person would desire, but through their courage and conservation, all single parents take all their troubles and the tough times to learn and make them more useful.

Apart from all their duties, *children need to see their parent happy*, not depressed, and your child will always see the hard work you put in. Though it is difficult, stop beating yourself up to do more, you are already doing your best, and that is all that matters. There are times you may think that you are not your best. However, each impediment you conquer will demonstrate how resilient and determined you are. In their kids' eyes, single parents turned into champions, but one frustrating problem is the prevalence of detrimental delusions.

Being a single parent is not an obstacle; you must own your single-parent status and find what you love and do it. Yes, you can be a single parent and make millions while raising your little ones. One crucial instrument for success in business is faith, and people can smell an absence of it on you. Start sturdy and self-fund by being a professional hustler and remember that working on a plan and problem-solving are both natural abilities for a productive parent entrepreneur. For me, I used to worry about money regularly, asking myself exactly how I start a business broke? I then chose to prove to the world that I can be a single mom and still have it all by establishing objectives for my business and my life. I was convinced that there are many single moms out there with exceptional encounters, so I decided to wear the hustler role and design work that is lucrative but not noticeable. The notion of pushing is not a new one. Thus, all the single mothers who are holding the strength and raising a family all by themselves, given the opportunity can start and maintain multi-million-dollar businesses.

Typically, being an entrepreneur is a formidable undertaking. However, there are so many men and women out there who are very profitable and still able to look after their children all by themselves. An uncommon goal involves an odd way of thinking that will take you outside your comfort zone, especially when you are broke. Use the knowledge of other people to help you, make a note of all the things that discourage you in your daily life, then research innovative approaches to tackle those inadequacies. Look for motivation everywhere: business coaches or whoever has the expertise that you might need; all it takes is a concept to generate a product that shifts the world. The search for the ideal work-life balance is what has delayed so many single moms from opening their businesses, therefore, be inclined to change because that's how you develop, whether you change your mindsets or your ambitions.

Raising kids alone can be strenuous; single parents manage work while trying to spend as much time with their kids as they can. Time and time again, lack of support is a reality for many, and looking for a balance between getting a babysitter or do something for yourself becomes an essential part of any parent's life. Society doesn't know what to do with single parents, as they have groups for every individual except single parents. However, the challenging parts about being a single mom for me have been the emotional struggles and insights that I've had to face. On good days and bad days, having a conscious heart to hear from God is crucial for the single mother who needs support, because there's great joy in seeing the hand of God in many miraculous ways and marvels.

Be cheerful and satisfied in life, instead of questioning what could have happened if the father was there, but instead, be grateful for your hard work bringing up your children. While it may sound complicated, it is also the shortcomings of life that give it strength, and that is how your children will see the love and know what attempts you are putting in for them.

Appreciate how amazing your children have turned out to be and pat yourself on the back. Of course, you will have your highs and lows, just look at the way you have brought up your children and consider that your children have you, and that is more than enough. Our tongue has so much influence over how our children see themselves, so I leaned into the word and applied it to my everyday life to shepherd me. There's no hesitation. It takes an incredible amount of power and audacity to raise kids on your own, but for the reality that single parents can function just as fine or even better than whole families are an achievement of itself.

In the first few weeks I became a single mom, I felt like I was dragged in a trillion different ways and trying to do everything on my own left my heart completely exhausted and my nerves on edge. My children and I were having daily breakdowns, and that was when I understood that being a single parent can make the most tolerant person lose their entire jar of marbles. Becoming a single mom wasn't a comfortable journey, but I had to discover that I have to manage and direct my children's hearts. I know we all make mistakes. I realized that it was difficult for me to endure without the spiritual tranquility and strength of Jesus. It's essential for me to every day to deliver my children's care to the Lord, and I knew that I could trust in God to keep his assurance and inspire me when I am feeling low.

While raising children alone can be a battle at times, I hold on to God's word, which gives me the power I need to keep pressing on. Being a single mom is not a handicap; instead of combating my conditions, I had to learn to acknowledge it. The Lord is a helper to give knowledge and vision on ministering to the children. He's accessible all the time to hear your prayers and act on your behalf. The Lord had always met all our needs, I learned to find happiness through Christ in the middle of a challenging position, and through the Holy Spirit, I will hear words of truth from the Bible to help me to keep pushing ahead. My heavenly Father is sympathetically keeping an eye on my children to achieve great things for the kingdom of God; thus, power in the present is the investment in my children that will reap a glorious return in the forthcoming.

A single parent raising children can find herself in a defenceless place, and of course, you must be strongly reliant on already strained social structures. The facts aren't great for the children of single parents, and this can be a very depressing statistic of life. Still, I believe God has angels to dispatch in my protection against hazardous people's circumstances. When a single mom is in harmony, so is her household because she has faith in their future, and God has a goal for every single mother's child.

Ban Toxic People from Your Life

When people hear that I am a single mom, it's like in their minds you cannot be effective, and these toxic effects are people who tell you that business is a big challenge and that you can't build anything valuable. Toxic influences are those people who always remind you that you are a single mom, and they have determined that because you're a single parent, you must be struggling. I couldn't change the reality that I was a single mom, but what I did is that I had to ban of all toxic influences who thinks that the only thing I should do is to raise my kids, but didn't help me how. For this reason, I am on a journey to break the stereotype of a single parent and all the depressing connotations correlated with it, not to worship around a toxic people. They overrun my faith and bring me down.

The most beautiful things in life are not worldly things, so don't confuse your life by surrounding yourself with people who see life as a contest rather than bringing a change in the world. Billy Graham once said, *"The greatest legacy one can pass on to one's children and grandchildren is not money or other material things accumulated in one's life, but rather a legacy of character and faith"* (Billy Graham, 2018). Some people will draw your attention to their lives so that you will be the one recruiting every opportunity for them, getting connections for them and once they get what they want from you, they will spit you out like chewing gum. So, choose your friends, be in the same lane with them because if you're not in the same class with your friends, you're might lose each other.

Occasionally a reliable best friend can be that neighbor who is the most supportive person ever. These days, a lot of people don't know their neighbors, yet friendly, reliable neighbors who have each other's backs are a fading breed. Friendships are more useful than just sharing laughs over a cup of coffee. Champions stand up for you and what you believe in because they are the friends who sing your praises. A paucity of strong relationships raises your probability of early grave. Therefore, both of you must devote time and resources to keeping the fire burning. Avoid keeping score, but if your social life is looking light, it might be time to make some new friends when you feel like you're the only one showing effort.

A true friend will continuously find a way to support you and care about what you're going through in life. Challenging circumstances uncover fake people in your life. When you need them the most, they will just vanish or else find an excuse. They will just hang around with you when they think you've got your life in order. Once you're in a mess, they say that you're on your own. Do you know that haters were once best friends? The spirit of a parasite shouldn't exit in friendships. Real friends can fix each other's crowns. Some friends are there, not for the sake of friendship. They are there to find how they can benefit from this person. A bond should always be a two-way street: if I contribute, you also contribute to my life. You shouldn't be the only one receiving. It is always advisable that you should choose your friends wisely, see who is of good value in your life, and if anybody doesn't add any value in your life, that is high time that you change your direction and pathways. Although the route is lengthy, there is no need hanging around people who always point you to the difficulties and not the way forward.

Although it's never a pleasant route to re-evaluate our own lives, it can be required to check-in from time to time, some friends are significant influences, always forcing you toward the finish line. They continuously invest in your growth and want you to be successful, even if self-reflection is needed for any sort of progress in our lives. These friends are generous with their time as they support you see your powers, so sit down with this person who will ask you the right kind of questions to better who you are. Real friends take pride in your relationship, and they will sacrifice for your gain, and you can count on them to recognize what you say without criticizing, even when others do not. Discovering the right work-life balance is a challenge every determined person faces. Still, it's entirely feasible to make time for friends who will always be there for you, whatever the conditions, and you share a practically resilient bond. Not all friendships need to be valuable past the point of enjoying each other's company, but everyone needs a non-judgmental friend who will help them no matter what. The people you surround yourself with have a significant influence on your life, so you need a friend who lets you be a hot mess and knows all of your deepest and darkest secrets, but still loves you all the same.

Don't worry about the adversary that attacks you, only a true friend will tell you to your face if something is not going well with your friendship, but be afraid of that fake acquaintance that cuddles you and can't share anything that others are saying behind your back. If you have a friend that you always give out but you don't receive anything back, or you have a friend where every time you'll be the one sharing information, and she's the one holding back, my friend think twice, that friend is using you. If you don't gain anything from your friendship, what's the point of hanging in there, because friends are supposed to build you up not to tear you down. I have considered myself to be this expensive piece of jewelry that is most of the time rejected because many can't afford it. I often get courage in declaring the greatness of God in my life by reading Psalms 27, "The LORD is my light and my salvation; Whom shall I fear? The LORD is the strength of my life; Of whom shall I be afraid? When the wicked came against me to eat up my flesh, My enemies and foes, They stumbled and fell" (Psalms 27:1-2 NKJV HolyBible, 2020). I urge you today not waste yourself in rejection or to even think that something is wrong with you, perhaps you're not good enough. Don't get disheartened from all the rejection, but instead count it as God's divine shield in the quest of success, to wake you up and get going to your fate.

Disappointment should not be our undertaker, but an opportunity to begin again, if you learn from it. Single parent, you must know what you want from life because you are solely accountable for your achievement and your disappointment. Remember that your dreams are valid, and all you need to do is fight for them, and the way you think about reality may beat you before you ever do anything about it. The earlier you understand that failure is a temporary deviation, then you'll keep on trying and build the right mindset. Accusing others of not achieving your goals in life can paralyze you and make your dreams challenging to meet, please handle disappointment with pride because you will not prosper in life without first failing.

NOTES

RISE LIKE A PHOENIX

Nompumelelo Real Kunene
CTC. SAM. TCP

- Strength is Built from Your Battles
- Be Accountable for Your Actions
- Don't be a Prisoner of Your Past
- Be a Pioneer for Your Future

RISE TO GREATER HEIGHTS

Nompumelelo Real Kunene
Nompumelelo Real Kunene

www.swaticanadianinternational.ca

Bonus 3

MAKE A DIFFERENCE TO THE VULNERABLE

Sometimes in life we go around complaining about everything: the weather is bad today, traffic was worse than expected, my family drives me crazy sometimes, the movie was disappointing, and you name it. Though whining can be a way to build inspiration, it also keeps us from acting and it gives excuses to procrastinate from achieving goals. One thing I've realized is that we usually complain in the wake of a negative situation, and we focus more on the problem rather than on potential solutions. It's always much easier to complain than to find a solution and individuals who whine on a regular basis are apt to have bad health.

Just be like this widow who never complained, even though she had every reason to complain, no one paid any attention. My mother suffered a double loss after my father died, the assets she could have inherited were taken by her in-laws. Being widowed presents a remarkable form of shift, one which is entirely different from any other kind of separation a human being can experience. She felt like the whole world was watching her so that they could sabotage any move she makes. You can only imagine how it felt being in her shoes, she just wished my dad had written a will to protect her from the inhuman mistreatment she got from his family members. Most of the treatment was geared towards dehumanizing her which was always a painful psychological experience that affected her throughout her life. My father had failed to write a will clearly stating how their assets would be distributed, this left my mom vulnerable to abuse from the in-laws. A story which is echoed in most societies. People generally avoid talking about death, yet death is inevitable, and when it's untimely it leaves such a devastating trail behind.

The moment she got married to my father, her dream of practising as a nurse was shattered, because of my grandmother who was so controlling. She remained a housewife, because according to my grandmother a married wife is only known to produce and raise children. My mom had to face reality, after losing her husband who was the sole provider in the family. The moment my mom was at her most vulnerable, she made choices that had an enduring impact on her wellbeing. She decided to stay in that compound through all the hardships. She decided to raise me and my four siblings as a single parent with no source of income, but with faith in God that he would meet all her needs. With the strength from above, she didn't give up on her children, she never gave up even when her mother-in-law never liked her. She stood up for what she believed in.

When your world comes crashing down, wear your scars with pride, to show how a phoenix feels when it dies inside and trust in your capability to soar from your own collapsed ruins. The Phoenix is a Greek mythological bird known to rise from its ashes after being buried hundred of years ago (Angela Michelle Schultz, 2019). This immortal creature acquires new life by rising from the ashes of its ancestor, which represents our capacity for vision, rebirth and success. Remember to put your vanity aside, have the confidence that you can always find how to deal with life, since the phoenix must burn first and experience pain before resurrection from its ashes. No matter what kind of obstacles life is subjecting you to, arise from that disaster, tougher and more effective. Don't be afraid to fall apart because strength is built from your battles, so believe in your ability to rise and do something you couldn't have done before, because God cannot give you anything you can't handle.

My mom had so much faith that one day she would see results of her perseverance, she believed that one day like the phoenix bird she would rise from the ashes. She also believed she would rise through those hardships, through those challenges, and through those persecutions. Today I call her my source of courage and a walking miracle. When I think of her, I'm often reminded of the book of Hebrews 11, "Now faith is the substance of things hoped for, the evidence of things not seen. For by it we obtained a good testimony. By faith we understand that the worlds were framed by the word of God, so that the things which are seen were not made of things which are visible" (Hebrews 11:1-3 NKJV BibleGateway, 2019).

My mom went from poverty and economic deprivation to marginalisation and inhuman treatment in my dad's family, in the church, as well as in the society. She has faced traumatic experiences in our community from the point of losing her husband. It was as if what happened to her is what everyone else was afraid of, so they just stared and prayed they wouldn't become like her one day. People tend to forget that widows are humans too, and as such they need fair treatment from members of the community. No matter what has happened to you in the past, I believe if you keep your faith in your abilities, work hard, determined and a faith in God, you can accomplish all your heart's desires.

Complaining doesn't resolve anything whatsoever, and you will never achieve happiness. The world doesn't owe you anything really, and you must be the one responsible for making a living. Do not let your situation take away the ability to see things in a more objective manner. Be accountable for your actions and responsibilities. Complaining isn't a solution, think about the individuals who wanted to see this day, but because their lives are not in their hands, they couldn't make it. In the meantime, you are complaining about the toilet seat that men don't put down after each bathroom visit. Next, you'll be complaining that, *"why does pizza come in square boxes, yet it is round, and funny enough it's cut in triangles"* (Unknown, 2020).

As a widow my mother instantly lost respect, her dignity, her voice and visibility as if everything which gave her rights to be human and a respected woman was attached to my father. Once he passed away, everything died with him, the love from his family, and the recognition. Strange how that happens huh? She became a misfit, back then when a woman lost her husband, she was required to wear black, and everyone would know that she was in mourning. It also made it obvious to everyone that she had no protector therefore rendering her vulnerable. I often think about the moment the whole community turned against her because she was wearing all black, and yet going through all that, she never complained. My mother stood for what she believed in, and she fought her battles in silence and prayer. She is the one who inspired us to be better women of today, she is the woman who made us realize that we can do business at a very tender age instead of waiting for a college degree. Not even a single day did I hear her complaining about what she was going through in life.

You can whine about the way your life is, but trust me, the world by now has enough whiners, all you need to do is act. Justifications are simply for those individuals who are reluctant to find solutions, but instead, they place blame on other people for their own actions. Be the one in charge of your driver's seat, be strict with yourself and take actions that carry you steadily forward to your achievement. Don't live in denial, your concerns can be born without involving everyone else in your own personal life. Do not waste precious moments that could be devoted to resolving matters that are distracting you from reaching your potential goals.

My mom is the one who stood by me and supported me whenever I couldn't see a way out. She would always bring solutions into my life and that's why I am the woman I am today She made me realize that I am capable of doing things exceedingly and abundantly well. Today I don't regret any circumstance that I went through in life, because through all those challenges, through all those circumstances, I came out even stronger and much better than before because I never lost faith.

I grew up as an orphan, a young girl with big dreams, back when big was all about the kings and queens. With the support of my mom, I knew exactly what I wanted in life. I would always go confidently in the direction of my dreams regardless of the challenges my mom faced while trying to provide for our basic needs. Even though at my school I was treated differently, and didn't fit anywhere, I never gave up because I knew that the God that is able to do all things exceedingly, will never ever give up on me and I continued to trust in his promises. Like a phoenix, I had the spirit within me that I was unstoppable in the pursuit of my dreams. I will rise above all odds and I won't give up because the God I serve is always on my side and, I'll always try to find a way of pulling out of each and every situation because the God within me is the God of possibilities.

I discovered that most orphans often become exposed to a host of psychological challenges as a result of their parents' death. Children who are deprived of parental care are more susceptible to psychological damaged and vulnerability. Emotional and social difficulties are more among orphans because the children would be differentiating their value of life as orphans, compared to the time when their parents were alive and well.

This rings true to my story. I faced many problems, including not having good friends because most of them measured life by material things which as you might guess I didn't have much of. As a result, they did not want to associate with me and that led to reduced social interaction. It contributed to continuous worries, isolation and other challenges. We lacked material resources, including food and clothes, and most of the time my mom would pay my school fees very late which always put me in the spotlight. I felt embarrassed, depressed and each time school term began I felt anxious. I was so fed up of being stigmatized, ignored and excluded from activities.

As an orphan growing up, within my community, I felt like I didn't belong there because most of the kids who had both parents, had all the things I couldn't afford. I told myself at a very tender age that the moment I became privileged, I wanted to make a difference in that community. To that orphan that didn't fit anywhere around the school, to that widow who couldn't belong anywhere in the community and whose voice had been silenced, that single parent who tried to raise children on their own. I wanted to give hope to those in hopeless situations, to remind them that they did exist and mattered in their communities. That they have a purpose to fulfil while they're still alive. I want to demonstrate the love of God to the vulnerable by giving back to the community.

Being a single mom is not easy, but you have to learn that life is a mix of the success and the failures, so learn to do impressive things just by following your heart and intuition. Most often I run into God's promises in the book of Isaiah 43: 1-2

"Don't be afraid, I've redeemed you. I've called your name. You're mine. When you're in over your head, I'll be there with you. When you're in rough waters, you will not go down. When you're between a rock and a hard place, it won't be a dead end— because I am God, your personal God" (Isaiah 43: 1-2 NKJV HolyBible, 2019).

We shouldn't be prisoners of our past since it's already passed, but we should be pioneers of our own future. We shouldn't be looking at what went wrong in our lives, but we should enjoy the present and focusing on what we can do better in our future. It doesn't matter what kind of circumstance you've gone through; you shouldn't let fear control you because it will destroy you. Fear will silence all your faith in trusting in God. Your situation today doesn't characterize your tomorrow. The life that you want to live in the future can start today, be convinced that your future is bright and continue in the direction of your aspirations.

From my experience as a single mom who grew up as an orphan and being raised by a widow, I never lost my faith and trust in God that he's always an omnipresent God watching over my life. I never lost faith that one day I would pull through that situation. You know, like a phoenix that rose from its ashes I believed that one day I would be successful. Different things happen to all of us, and you can make decisions that will keep you in prison for the rest of your life or be a pioneer of your future. It doesn't matter how many years had been wasted chasing life in the opposite direction, but I knew that one day my time would come, because I was not living somebody else's life, but I was living the life that God had purposed for me. I believe in what I can do, not focusing on the mistakes I've made, because the mistakes will be the ones that will pave a way for me. The only thing

I can do is to learn from my mistakes, and I am moving forward in life because I see a brighter future beyond the tunnel.

I've learnt that single parenting is one task that comes with a responsibility like no other job, it's not a job for the timid.

- It's right that parenting is a ride that goes easier with two parents, it requires a lot of confidence and determination. It also helps to create one of the strongest bonds in the world.
- Though being a single mom is an uncertain and challenging job and perhaps one which has no retreat, your children will see the effort you put in, so just pull through to provide a happy life for their kids.
- Make sure your children are your priority, they will see you do great and they will also see you fail at times, this will teach them that life has got ups and downs.
- When you take up the task alone and have to play double the duties, you then realize what value you must give to your children and how precious that time with them is.
- If you are a solo parent, the duties are always bigger than your capability, but all of it will only make your relationship with your children stronger if done right, and you will see what an amazing job you have done.

Even though all mothers deal with emotions of remorse, being a single parent is not easy, you try so hard to divide your time to fulfill all your duties as a mother and a working woman. In fact, I am learning that, as a single mom there is even more pressure because I strive to give the best to my kids, and I am also determined to show other single parents that it is possible to be a success. My whole life has changed forever, being a single mom is a new chapter in my life that doesn't imply that is the end of my ambitions, but to look for more opportunities out there to give my kids the best life possible.

I believe in promoting poverty relief and community empowerment to others who are impoverished in society, so that the less privileged individuals have their basic needs met in order to improve economic opportunities to impact their community. I founded Swazi Canadian International Foundation, to stimulate world-wide awareness and availing resources on the dilemma of those trapped in a series of poverty; convey confidence to the vulnerable; strive to alleviate the suffering; illiteracy; and to build a dependable network in making sure that our commitment of better life for all is achieved in a compassionate and dignified manner.

We can make a difference in this world that we live in, if we can just be kind to everybody we come across. Kindness can change everything because one really doesn't know what the other person is going through. I want to encourage you by letting you know that when something poses as an obstacle to you, that situation challenges you to discover the ability to press forward. Actual strength is in the hands of the one who flourishes and there's hope for your situation, so utilize it as a marvel to step on to a better view.

NOTES

RESILIENCE
to
GREATNESS
Learn from Pain
Be inclined to build resilience
Stay dedicated to what matters the most
Build External Resources
You are destined for greatness
Nompumelelo Real Kunene
Nompumelelo Real Kunene
www.swaticanadianinternational.ca
Nompumelelo Real Kunene

Bonus 4

RESILIENCE TO GREATNESS

You are destined for greatness, and it is our confidence in God that can push us in the direction of accomplishing the difficult. Inside of you, God has put seeds of excellence, and the mystery to achieving it is basically to do every insignificant thing in a good approach. Those seeds are to grow and flourish if you're prepared to break out into a more substantial opportunity. It takes a whole lot of ambling to come up with the theory, and for us to decide that we are destined for greatness is we must make the right determination that will bring us to our future. Many people have become crippled by their past encounters; some have barrelled over other people to get to the top. Overall, I believe that God has a plan for every one of us. Your objective is what you were designed for and the reason why you live.

I have seen the attitude to hardship play out in all walks of life and realized that resilience is the signature of excellence. Every great leader worth their pinch was strong; stories of struggle often become experiences in how to stay resilient. They believed in a source more significant than themselves and were constant to accomplish their goals. They defined themselves by influence and awkward encounters but have been able to surmount them. Entrepreneurship is a journey full of lessons and many bounces along the way, but discovering our reason is the most crucial objective of life, with a vigorous dosage of resilience. For this reason, there is something admirable about people who keep fighting for their dreams no matter what barriers they face. They have the strength to thrive, which is the energy you need to get through difficult situations.

Here are five keys to focus on to create a better level of resiliency and ensure you stay unruffled by turmoil and ambiguity. With these ways, we can deal with our battles a lot better and reframe strength as a close friend instead of a ferocious adversary.

1. Learn from pain - when you are going through difficult times, it is easy to lose our cool. However, we need to learn the most from the pain and rethink what's required to be effective. We will face battles at times, heart-wrenching instants, but utilizing what we've discovered from the discomfort will help us to be able to control whatever comes our way.
2. Be inclined to build resilience - some of our challenges will trigger us to develop in some way, thus, learning to deal with and tackle hardship is what creates resilience. Every problem we encounter strengthens our capability to overcome future hurdles, so we can learn to be comfortable in a difficult situation by taking new risks.
3. Stay dedicated to what matters most- our struggles can frequently put things in a better viewpoint, and defeating such hardship is character building. You must keep your moods up despite harsh conditions, and your resilience will improve only with high energy. We always have the option to change our focus on what we want. It generates the learning tools to deal with the issues that don't go our direction.
4. Build external resources - hard times helps us find a friend; we need people for emotional and psychological encouragement. During stressful moments, you will be amazed at how often someone will have had a comparable experience, and these are people who can lighten us up when we're not at our best. Establishing a solid support group can help steer you through a challenging moment, and our peer

group can guide us to continue resilient and focus on what's going right.
5. Accept it---we will never soar higher than the beliefs we have for ourselves if we acknowledge that hardship is unavoidable. Any great leader always anticipates winning even when they are failing, so better yet accept it as a pure reward on the road to getting better.

Resilience is the incredibly core of each of our excellence, and it is the knowledge that comes from it that generates the opportunity for development. It can bring out your good or bad, but it's from these areas when we produce the most. Misfortune plays a crucial part in the evolution and the final vital element when creating a business that passionately drives a transformation. As seen, resilience is one of the most influential forces in life that challenges you to the foundation where your capability to rebound is built.

From the beginning of time until today, people have been clutching for prominence. For us to go from the bottom of the steps to the pinnacle of the stairs, we merely need to take a step. Simply work towards achieving your fullest ability as a human being by setting out to achieve your vision when the timing is perfect! A life of greatness is what God desires for each one of us and the gifts we must allow us to serve one another as human beings. *Greatness comes from depending solely on God*, and he appears to delight in taking those who are of less importance to the world and transforming them into inspirational leaders. As expressed, God has a plan for you, and his wish is for you to be so full of his anointing that it bursts to others.

Any man in Christ is intended for greatness. Our tranquillity comes from the truth that Jesus traded the grandeur of heaven for the dust of the earth. The peace that we have as Christians streams out of the detriment that Jesus made on our behalf, and we can have confidence in God even when we have doubts that we are the chosen ones. God takes the least of men and makes them great, but if we attempt to become great through our endeavors, we will ultimately not succeed. One of the things that excite me about the way God works is that it is only through following his approach of doing things that we can achieve greatness in our life. Greatness in Jesus' eyes is fulfilling the needs of others. This is the right path to greatness by blessing the lives of many others around you. With God, we are destined for greatness as we follow his strategy, this is when the growth commences because discovering your gift and following God's idea will show you what your reason in life is.

NOTES

REFERENCES

Berry, Halle. "Halle Berry thinks work makes her a better mother ." 27 July 2017. *AP News.* <https://apnews.com/23f2b71a4a204ab7bc7107776c389ad7>.

Brown, Les. 18 April 2020. *Quote Fancy.* <https://quotefancy.com/quote/853110/Les-Brown-We-must-look-for-ways-to-be-an-active-force-in-our-own-lives-We-must-take>.

Caine, Christine. "Quotable Quote." 13 January 2016. *Good Reads.* <https://www.goodreads.com/quotes/7072229-sometimes-when-you-re-in-a-dark-place-you-think-you-ve>.

Elizabeth, Queen. "Queen Elizabeth's Most Delightful, Witty, and Moving Quotes." 19 August 2018. *Town and Country.* <https://www.townandcountrymag.com/society/tradition/a22630274/queen-elizabeth-quotes/>.

Graham, Billy. "Billy Graham: The greatest legacy – Generosity Monk." 23 February 2018. *Generosity Monk.* <https://generositymonk.com/2018/02/23/billy-graham-the-greatest-legacy/>.

HolyBible. 7 April 2020. *www.bible.com.* <https://www.bible.com/bible/114/psa.56.3.nkjv>.

Jakes, Bishop T.D. "20+ T.D. Jakes Quotes On Leadership." 2020. *Christian Quotes Bro.* <https://www.christianquotesbro.com/TD-Jakes-quotes-leadership.html>.

Lindell, Debbie. "A 31-Day Journey to Confident Conversations with God." 2019. *Google Books.* <https://books.google.ca/books?id=ZAelDwAAQBAJ&pg=PT86&lpg=PT86&dq=Debbie+Lindell:+Even+when+you+cannot+see+the+future,+you+can+know+that+God+is+already+there.&source=bl&ots=ftkeL_gzSO&sig=ACfU3U1HMblCauUqwSLZk4uFWj91dLBHpA&hl=en&sa=X&ved=2ahUKEwioueOigvjo>.

Mandela, Nelson. "Long Walk to Freedom: The Autobiography of Nelson Mandela." 2008. *Google Books.* <https://books.google.ca/books?id=RHwLqVrnXgIC&printsec=frontcover&dq=nelson+mandela+May+your+choices+refle

ct+your+hopes,+not+your+fears&hl=en&sa=X&ved=0ahUK
EwjAwoOYlv_oAhWDvp4KHd_mAXcQ6AEIKDAA#v=one
page&q&f=false>.
Obama, Barack. "Obama at Black Caucus dinner: "I need your help"." 24 September 2011. *CBS News.* <https://www.cbsnews.com/news/obama-at-black-caucus-dinner-i-need-your-help/>.
Obama, Michelle. "Remarks by The First lady at "Change Direction" Mental Health Event." 4 March 2015. *The White House.* <https://obamawhitehouse.archives.gov/the-press-office/2015/03/04/remarks-first-lady-change-direction-mental-health-event>.
Schultz, Angela Michelle. "The Phoenix: A Mythological Bird." 13 February 2019. *OWLCATION.* <https://owlcation.com/humanities/Phoenix-Bird>.
Shelton, Trent. "Trent Shelton." 25 June 2015. *Good Reads.* <https://www.goodreads.com/quotes/7107729-we-are-all-a-little-broken-but-last-time-i>.
Shirer, Priscilla. "Awaken: 90 Days with the God Who Speaks." 2011. *Google Books.* <https://books.google.ca/books?id=S5UtDwAAQBAJ&pg=PT209&lpg=PT209&dq=Every+decision+you+need+to+make,+every+task+you+need+to+accomplish,+every+relationship+you+need+to+navigate,+every+element+of+daily+life+you+need+to+traverse,+God+has+already+perfectly+ma>.
TerKeust, Lysa. "Uninvited: Living Loved When You Feel Less Than, Left Out and Lonely." 2016. <https://books.google.ca/books?id=GxnxCgAAQBAJ&pg=PA23&lpg=PA23&dq=The+mind+feasts+on+what+it+focuses+on.+What+consumes+my+thinking+will+be+the+making+or+the+breaking+of+my+identity&source=bl&ots=KKd2YnOu1f&sig=ACfU3U24bfmgYllYLidINlbK7Iv2Qp-RLA&hl=en&sa=X>.
Trudeau, Justin. "Justin Trudeau: The Natural Heir." 2016. *Google Books.* <https://books.google.ca/books?id=cKvrCgAAQBAJ&pg=PT135&dq=I+have+no+regrets.+Justin+Trudeau&hl=en&sa=X

&ved=0ahUKEwj36_P_lv_oAhWAIDQIHY9EC-cQ6AEIKDAA#v=onepage&q=I%20have%20no%20regrets.%20Justin%20Trudeau&f=false>.

Trump, Donald. "Trump's official inauguration." 12 February 2017. *The Hill.* <https://thehill.com/blogs/blog-briefing-room/news/319170-trumps-official-inauguration-poster-has-glaring-typo>.

Unknown. n.d.

Winfrey, Oprah. "23 Leadership Tips From Oprah Winfrey." 27 September 2012. *Forbes.* <https://www.forbes.com/sites/johngreathouse/2012/09/27/23-leadership-tips-from-oprah-winfrey/#711e0f921a5d>.

ABOUT THE AUTHOR

NOMPUMELELO REAL KUNENE, PhD
Human Rights Analyst * Motivational Speaker *
#1 Bestselling Author * Mentor * Life and Business Coach *
Serial Entrepreneur * Trainer *
CEO of Swati Canadian international Corp.
www.swaticanadianinternational.ca
HOST of RISE TO GREATER HEIGHTS NETWORK
www.risetogreaterheights.com
ALBERTA, CANADA

Born in the Kingdom of ESWATINI, Dr. Nompumelelo Real Kunene is a highly sought after energetic certified Les Brown International speaker. Real is also a PhD graduate – Leadership and Business, coach, mentor, and an emcee, well known for encouraging many to rise from mediocrity into greatness. She is an Amazon #1 6x bestselling and an International Bestselling author of Rise to Greater Heights and Human Rights-God Given Fundamental Freedoms Books, as well as a compiler for Resilience to Greatness and Cultivate Your Mindset for Success, What's Holding You Back and Equal in Dignity books, to turn your fears into greater success while seizing new opportunities. Her vision is not only to motivate but also to empower audiences with a fresh perspective inspiration they require to pursue success and drive sustainable outcomes, in a seriously funny way. Dr. Kunene's mission is to meet the needs and transform lives of her clients and her audience. Her book "Rise to Greater Heights" has inspired and empowered many to pursue their personal and professional passion to become go-getters. Dr. Kunene's goal is to: study your current situation, identify limiting beliefs, then design a plan of inspired action to empower you to achieve specific outcomes in your life. Dr. Real Kunene wears many hats, as a CEO, Bestselling Author, Strategist, Trainer, Philanthropist, Diplomacy Protocol Officer, International Human Rights Analyst and a Commissioner for Oaths, following her dreams gave her purpose to see her goals through and understand that she does have everything she needs to reach her full potential. Hebrews 11, Psalms 27 and 40, keeps her to rise to greater heights.

BOOK Dr. Real N. Kunene FOR YOUR NEXT EVENT
Tel: +1(780) 803-5891
admin@risetogreaterheights.com
www.risetogreaterheights.com

TESTIMONIALS: https://risetogreaterheights.com/testimonials/

Connect with Dr. Real N. KUNENE daily:
Website: www.risetogreaterheights.com
E-mail: admin@risetogreaterheights.com
Facebook: Nompumelelo Real Kunene https://www.facebook.com/RisetoGreaterHeights/
Instagram: Nompumelelo Real Kunene https://www.instagram.com/rise_to_greater_heights/
YouTube: Nompumelelo Real Kunene https://youtube.com/channel/UCoHaIVC9Y-jSb8b5n--XQhQ
LinkedIn https://www.linkedin.com/in/nompumelelo-real-kunene
Consultation: https://risetogreaterheights.com/book-a-consultation/
Event Booking: https://risetogreaterheights.com/speaker-publisher/
Book : https://risetogreaterheights.com/book-community-magazine/
SPEAKING TOPICS:

1. **What's Holding you Back?**
2. **Chase After Success**
3. **Grow Your Business**
4. **Overcome Business Obstacles**
5. **Secrets to Achieve Work-Life Balance**
6. **Cultivate Your Mindset | Transformation**
7. **Mental Heath | Emotional Intelligence**
8. **Leadership | Empowerment**
9. **Mentorship and Coaching**
10. **Strategies to Grow Your Church**
11. **Ways to Trust GOD**
12. **Tips on Successful Single Parenting**
13. **Make a Difference to the Vulnerable**
14. **Resilience to Greatness**
15. **Human Rights**
16. **Diplomacy and Protocol**

Dr. Nompumelelo Real Kunene is a CERTIFIED TRAVEL COUNSELLOR (CTC) and a member in good standing in the Association of Canadian Travel Agencies (ACTA) and subscribes to its Code of Ethics which require that a member's relationship with the public and the travel industry to be of a high standard. Her goal is to make incremental adjustments to her everyday life, so she uncovered varied opportunities to see what sticks and what doesn't. Real has achieved the highest level of recognition as a Professional Certified SALES MANAGER (SAM, TCP) through mastery of the expertise and skills in the National Occupational Standards established by the Canadian Tourism Industry. The reality is, her journey to be a better person started with her, she made the change from being an idle bum to someone who act.

Being a HUMAN RIGHTS ANALYST, Dr. Kunene believes that you really don't have to be politically involved to learn about your human rights. All human beings are entitled to them, and you can never ever be prohibited from your own HUMAN RIGHTS. These are God given fundamental rights and freedoms! Human rights are not just about the law; thus, human rights are non-discriminatory... meaning that all human beings are entitled to them! She believes that we need to challenge ourselves to turn our resilience into our platform to be true advocates for all human rights. It doesn't matter where we are born or what kind of a family we are born into, we all have the internal recognition of the moral quality of one's motives and actions.

Following her dreams gave her purpose to see her goals through and understand that she does have everything she needs to reach her full potential. Pursuant to the Notaries and Commissioners Act, Part 2, Section 15, KUNENE, Nompumelelo Real has been appointed by the Minister of Justice and Solicitor General to be a Commissioner for Oaths in and for the Province of Alberta. She complies with the highest standards of behaviour as set out in the Notaries and Commissioners Act and the Commissioners for Oaths Regulation. Dr. Kunene is authorized by the Notaries and Commissioners Act. Section 19 to administer statutory declarations, affidavits, oaths and affirmations to establish legal rights.

Nompumelelo is the author of the book titled "RISE TO GREATER HEIGHTS" where Les Brown (world leading motivational speaker and trainer) wrote the foreword. "Hi my name is Les Brown international motivational speaker and trainer. I highly recommend Rise to Greater Heights for entrepreneurs, executives and professionals. Dr. Kunene is a powerhouse of a young lady. I really respect her tenacity and determination in taking charge of her destiny. It has been said that success leaves clues. Nompumelelo has shared the many lessons she has learned along her road to success as an entrepreneur. ~ LES BROWN" Rise to Greater Heights Book is a comprehensive guide to turn your fears into greater success while seizing new opportunities. Setting your mindset for success is significant, thus, this book has the potential to completely revolutionize every aspect of your life and career. Nompumelelo being mentored and coached by Les Brown (with his high-impact, customized message and standing ovation), she has been motivated and trained to be an achiever and leader with the mentality of Not Over Until You Win, Up Thoughts for Down Times and Fight For Your Dream.

Real has established a strong foundation as a Certified Mentor Coach by: learning industry best practices, helping her clients live passionate and meaningful lives and discover their greater life purpose, old programming empowering them to unleash their happiness from within, instilling the 4-Steps to Goal Success in their lives because she believes that all success depends on achieving meaningful goals by having a solid short and long term plan. She has mastered training in life purpose, business professional, millennial Mentorship, happiness, goal attainment, market goal and purpose coaching with Sales Presentation Blueprint and coaching methodologies.

Knowing that not everything in life is straight and easily done, she is eager to take an opportunity and push herself outside of her comfort zone. After learning and mastering the art of make-up application, their ingredients and effect on the skin, Nompumelelo decided to combine her passions for makeup artistry and skincare by becoming a licensed Medical Aesthetician.

Letting go of undesirable opinions allowed her to turn out to be the best version of herself which helped her to heal emotionally and gave her peace. Nompumelelo is also the CEO and Founder of Swati Canadian International and Swazi Canadian International Foundation, which is worldwide humanitarian relief and development organization dedicated to support the less privileged with basic needs through communities, churches and schools in order to create a more just and balanced world by bringing hope and tangible help. Being a philanthropist, her objective is to demonstrate the love of God and promote poverty relief and community empowerment in developing countries through relief and development projects. She is an advocate for the vulnerable and a voice for the less privileged. Building solid, consistent habits withstood her through lackluster eras to shake things up in her life. As she is going through life and working towards her dreams, she makes sure to position herself on a track to becoming who she really wants to be.

Rise to Greater Heights
Nompumelelo Real Kunene
CTC, SAM, TCP
Business
School
Community
Church
Professional Speaker | Author | MentorCoach | eMCee
Certified SALES MANAGER | CEO | Entrepreneur
Certified Travel Counsellor | Aesthetician
Philanthropist | Commissioner for Oaths
SPEAKING TOPICS:
What's Holding you Back?
Chase After Success
Grow Your Business
Overcome Business Obstacles
Secrets to Achieve Work-Life Balance
Cultivate Your Mindset
Mental Heath | Emotional Intelligence
Leadership | Empowerment
Mentorship and Coaching
Strategies to Grow Your Church
Ways to Trust GOD
Tips on Successful Single Parenting
Make a Difference to the Vulnerable
Resilience to Greatness
BOOK NOMPUMELELO
FOR YOUR NEXT EVENT
E-mail: ceo@swaticanadianinternational.ca
Tel: +1(780) 803-5891
www.swaticanadianinternational.ca

NOTES

RESOURCES

www.risetogreaterheights.com
www.swaticanadianinternational.ca

EQUAL IN DIGNITY
Human Rights
GOD GIVEN FUNDAMENTAL RIGHTS AND FREEDOMS
DR.NOMPUMELELO REAL KUNENE
EQUAL IN DIGNITY - HUMAN RIGHTS
EQUAL IN DIGNITY
Human Rights
GOD GIVEN FUNDAMENTAL RIGHTS AND FREEDOMS
Compiled By
DR.NOMPUMELELO REAL KUNENE
EQUAL IN DIGNITY
GOD GIVEN FUNDAMENTAL RIGHTS AND FREEDOMS
EQUAL IN DIGNITY
Human Rights
GOD GIVEN FUNDAMENTAL RIGHTS AND FREEDOMS
Compiled By
DR.NOMPUMELELO REAL KUNENE

CULTIVATE YOUR MINDSET FOR SUCCESS
RISE TO GREATER HEIGHTS
Nompumelelo R. Kunene - CTC, SAM, TCP

RESILIENCE TO GREATNESS
RESILIENCE TO GREATNESS - RISE TO GREATER HEIGHTS
RESILIENCE TO GREATNESS

HUMAN
RIGHTS
GOD GIVEN
FUNDAMENTAL FREEDOMS
RELIGION
OPINION
freedom
ASSOCIATION
CULTURE
ENGAGE
Nompumelelo R. Kunene - CTC, SAM, TCP
HUMAN RIGHTS
GOD GIVEN FUNDAMENTAL FREEDOMS
HUMAN
RIGHTS
freedom

RISE TO GREATER HEIGHTS
RISE TO GREATER HEIGHTS
LEADERSHIP-PURPOSE DRIVEN-EMOTIONAL INTELLIGENCE
RISE TO GREATER HEIGHTS
RISE TO GREATER HEIGHTS
LEADERSHIP-PURPOSE DRIVEN-EMOTIONAL INTELLIGENCE